purezza

VEGAN PIZZA

VEGAN PIZZA

DELICIOUSLY SIMPLE PLANT-BASED PIZZA TO MAKE AT HOME

Filippo Rosato, Tim Barclay and Stefania Evangelisti

Photography by Faith Mason

KYLE BOOKS

To little Leonardo and the future generations who can learn from the early years of their lives to love and respect the planet, to educate and inspire people to eat plant-based food for the animals, for the environment and for their health, and to make the world a better place for all.

An Hachette UK Company
www.hachette.co.uk

First published in Great Britain in 2020 by
Kyle Books, an imprint of Kyle Cathie Ltd
Carmelite House
50 Victoria Embankment
London EC4Y 0DZ
www.kylebooks.co.uk

ISBN: 9780857837448

Publisher: Joanna Copestick
Editorial Director: Judith Hannam
Editor: Tara O'Sullivan
Editorial Assistant: Florence Filose
Design: Paul Palmer-Edwards
Photography: Faith Mason
Food styling: Emily Jonzen
Props styling: Agathe Gits
Production: Allison Gonsalves

A Cataloguing in Publication record for this title is available from the British Library.

Printed and bound in China

10 9 8 7 6 5 4 3 2 1

Contents

INTRODUCTION

It's funny how, when you think about it, every restaurant across the world was born from nothing but ideas and dreams. Purezza was no exception to this, but the dreams and ideas that the restaurant stemmed from were remarkable. The goal was to create a revolutionary way of doing Italian cuisine. To modernise the concept of pizza. To reformulate and rebuild it in a way that's better for human health, the health of the planet and the health of the beings we share the planet with. To create the UK's first plant-based pizzeria.

The restaurant was the brainchild of partners Tim Barclay and Stefania Evangelisti, experts in plant-based dining, as well as Filippo Rosato, an expert in Neapolitan pizza. As a team, we worked tirelessly, perfecting key elements of the Neapolitan heritage, such as traditional sourdough, whilst also innovating animal-based ingredients that were traditionally used, in order to create plant-based alternatives. Our first restaurant opened in Brighton in 2015.

Those dreams and ideas never went away. They were baked into the very fabric of the restaurant, and the team never stopped researching - and this still continues today. Innovation after innovation came out of this. Plant-based mozzarella that acts and tastes like dairy, but with half the fat and no allergens. Vegan meats that contain a fraction of the saturated fat but taste identical to their animal-based counterparts. A range of delicious, health-enriched sourdough and standard pizza doughs, as well as a gluten-free version that's indistinguishable from the traditional Neapolitan dough.

The philosophy that Purezza adopted was that of Plant Pioneers. If an animal product was used in Italian cooking, we worked out how to recreate it using plants. Where other restaurants have made 'vegetarian' or 'vegan' a cuisine in and of itself, we have always been an Italian restaurant. We just make the food with plants alone.

Italian cuisine has a rich heritage. Depending on your definition, pizza dates back at least hundreds of years, if not millennia. It has seen many changes and evolutions throughout its time. The first true pizzeria opened in 1830. The birth of the Margherita, the world's most popular pizza (and the one that made cheese a central part of pizza tradition), was in 1889. New York's Italian community provided their own recipes throughout the early 1900s, crafting the pepperoni and meatball pizza. Throughout the twentieth century, the pizza went from being a niche Italian dish to a worldwide food phenomenon.

The food in this book is the latest innovation in pizzas, as well as in Italian cuisine. Paying homage to pizza's Neapolitan heritage, and yet changing and modernising for a new world, this is Italian food at the best it's ever been. This is its future. We hope you enjoy pioneering, cooking and eating these dishes as much as we enjoyed creating them.

WHY WE WROTE THIS BOOK

Our customers at Purezza ask one question more than any other: How do I make this at home? Be it about our cheeses, our pizzas, our desserts or any of our other dishes. This book is structured in a way that makes it easy. You'll build your own pizzas from the ground up, starting with making your very own sourdough, standard or gluten-free pizza dough. We then share cheeses, sauces, toppings and more.

The dishes presented here are amongst our favourite recipes. They feature numerous classics from our restaurants, including the Parmigiana Pizza, which won the National Pizza of the Year award in 2018.

Start by making some of our suggested pizzas, but after you try them all out we highly encourage you to follow your Plant Pioneer instincts too and experiment with different ideas. Whilst this book contains all the recipes that our restaurant customers have asked for, it's really up to you as to how you apply them. Our hope is that you become an ambassador for a new, modern way of crafting Italian cuisine, and we hope our book will be your guide.

A FEW NOTES...
A soya-free book
At Purezza, we want recipes that everyone can enjoy, regardless of dietary choices, restrictions and allergies. Whilst it's not the primary reason for creating plant-based foods, with dairy being one of the largest allergens in the world, we're proud to be able to serve the millions of people who suffer from milk allergies and lactose intolerance.

Due to this, we have also avoided using soya. Whilst not as impactful as dairy, soya is still a major allergen, and we made a decision early on to avoid using it.

As such, you won't find soya in this book. Where a recipe calls for plant-based milks, you can choose to use soya, but we find nut milks, rice milk and oat milk are great replacements.

All recipes are available gluten-free
We have also made it simple to remove gluten from all recipes. We have provided a recipe for gluten-free pizza dough, which tastes just as good as its counterpart, meaning it's a simple and straight swap for most pizzas.

Where gluten is used, it is marked in the recipe, meaning you can simply omit the ingredient or swap it for a suitable gluten-free replacement.

Pink Himalayan salt
Wherever a recipe uses salt, we call for pink Himalayan salt. This salt has a pink tinge, which certainly makes it look more aesthetically attractive, but it's the health benefits we're interested in. Himalayan salt provides a wealth of vital minerals to the body when it's consumed, turning a relatively unhealthy addition to food into a healthy component of dishes that use it. Pink Himalayan salt is now widely available and easy to obtain. It's a little more expensive, but we don't think you can put a price on your health.

EQUIPMENT

The greatest mind that Italy ever produced was Leonardo da Vinci. Famed for his art as much as his scientific discoveries, da Vinci was a true polymath and genius, but also a follower of a meat-free diet. The food that we are going to create can be viewed as a form of art. Its purpose is to delight the senses, from the bright and vibrant tones of Italian vegetables, to the aromas that'll fill your kitchen and dining room, and last but not least the flavours that you'll savour on your tongue. The process for creating our food is decidedly scientific, and any scientist needs their apparatus. We advise stocking your kitchen with the following tools. They'll weigh the ingredients, shape the compounds, and combine the components in a scientific manner, and through science we'll create art in the form of food. Here are the things you'll need...

Bowl
A large ceramic bowl with a capacity of approximately 2 litres is perfect. All of our pizza recipes are designed to feed four people, and this is just the right size to mix the dough in.

Scales
Weighing out this, that and the other ingredients is made simple with a high-quality set of scales. These are so essential that we recommend spending a little more here. A good-quality set will last you for years, a bad-quality set will produce recipes that are slightly off due to mismeasured ingredients. Digital or nondigital is fine.

Precision Scales
Another set of scales, but this time a precision set. These can detect tiny alterations in weight, which make them extremely useful for adding smaller quantities of ingredients to recipes.

Dough Ball Containers
During proving, dough balls should be stored in a tray-like container. There are multiple options here, from professional to basic. We recommend looking for something basic, as professional versions are designed for restaurants and are often very large. We also recommend opting for hardwood over plastic, as it allows the dough to breathe and keeps a more natural moisture level. Both of these are better than a commonly used alternative metal baking tray, as they provide much better insulation and warmth to the dough.

Pizza Stone
A pizza stone is typically made of ceramic or stone and is the most effective method of cooking pizzas in a domestic oven. Slotting this into your home oven will provide the perfect stage for pizzas to cook on, allowing them to get to exceptionally high temperatures and creating a crisper dough, as the stone will draw some moisture out of the pizza as it cooks.

Pizza Peel
A pizza peel will help you get pizza into and out of your oven with minimal fuss. It will protect the dough from changing shape and generally make life easier for you. There's a lot of debate about whether wood or metal pizza peels are better. We'd say that both types work great as long as you sprinkle them with a generous amount of flour before use.

Deep-fat Fryer or Large Pan
Some of the pizzas, such as our Montanara, are actually cooked in a deep-fat fryer. In addition, some of our favourite toppings in this book are simpler to make if you have one to hand. This provides unparalleled flavour and texture. For those who can't invest in a deep-fat fryer, however, a large pan or wok will provide a good substitute.

Skimmer
A skimmer is a large, slotted spoon. It's designed for deep-frying, and enables you to carefully move foods in the deep-fat fryer or frying pan around, ensuring that they become uniformly cooked all over. The slots stop the oil from splashing around, and you can remove food from the oil easily.

Thermometer
We highly recommended using a thermometer for managing and creating the perfect sourdough. A basic household or kitchen thermometer will do.

Dough Scraper

Dough balls can be sticky, and they grow during fermentation, meaning they tend to end up sticking together. A dough scraper (usually made of plastic or stainless steel) will handle all of this, allowing you to slice away dough balls that are to be used, as well as pick them up with no fuss.

Measuring Spoons

An essential piece of kit for making our recipes is a set of measuring spoons, which can be easily sourced online or at your local supermarket. They come in sets, usually between four and six. This includes ¼, ½ and 1 teaspoon and 1 tablespoon. These are not to be confused with cutlery, though - cutlery spoons are not standardised and frequently hold somewhat less than their measuring spoon counterparts.

Spoons

A variety of cooking spoons can be useful. We recommend one large spoon or ladle for scooping out and spreading sauce across pizzas, as well as one with slots, which makes it easy to separate liquid from your dishes. You may also want to invest in a spaghetti spoon, which makes it easier to serve up some of the pasta dishes in this book.

Measuring Jug

Our recipes include liquid ingredients, therefore a measuring jug will come in handy.

Whisk

Some of our recipes involve cooking several separate components before combining them to create the final dish. A simple whisk makes it easier to combine liquid ingredients together and will save you time.

Handheld Blender or Food Processor

A handheld blender or food processor will make your sauce-making dreams come true. Allowing you to quickly and efficiently blend various components for sauces, this will have vegetables turned into creamy toppings for your dough in a matter of seconds.

Blender or High-speed Blender

For some of the recipes, there are so many components to blend that a handheld blender simply won't do. A larger countertop blender or high-speed blender (especially useful for some of the 'cheese' recipes that contain nuts) will be ideal for this, allowing you to simply pour various ingredients in, hit a button, and have a sauce or 'cheese' ready before you can say 'mamma mia!'

Baking Tray

A baking tray is necessary for some of the toppings. A good metal one is perfect here, and will conduct heat, meaning it'll be cooking whatever's on it evenly throughout.

CHAPTER 1

DOUGH

A great pizza starts with a great base. So often we find that pizzerias and pizza chefs talk proudly about their recipes and their chosen toppings, but neglect where it all begins. But if you opened a pizzeria in Naples, the home of pizza, without being completely 'doughbsessed', they'd laugh you out of the city. Here's how to get it right, whether you choose to make your own sourdough, a quick and easy wholemeal base for when you're in a hurry, or a gluten-free dough.

WHOLEMEAL DOUGH

- NEAPOLITAN STYLE -

A traditional Neapolitan-style pizza comes with a thin base and a puffy, airy crust – a combination that makes pizza light and soft in texture. At Purezza, we mix the common 'O' or 'OO' flour with a blend of wholemeal flour to give the pizza a more rustic and authentic flavour.

This dough will take 8 hours to mature, so it can be prepared in the evening for lunchtime the next day or in the morning for the evening. It is important to choose a flour that contains around 11-12g of protein in each 100g to enable the dough to ferment and mature in 8 hours. This information can be found on the nutrition label.

The ideal ambient (room) temperature to allow the dough to ferment is 20-23°C. If the ambient temperature is lower, then we suggest using 0.6g of dry yeast instead of 0.5g to allow the dough to still mature within the 8 hours.

With this recipe you will be able to produce four dough balls of 200g each, ready to be used after the maturation is complete. However, they can also be stored in the fridge for up to 1 day or frozen for up to 1 month. To freeze, place the dough balls in the freezer as soon as they are made, before maturation. When you're ready to use them, allow at least 12 hours for defrosting at room temperature.

MAKES ENOUGH DOUGH FOR 4 PIZZAS

450g strong white bread flour, plus extra
    for dusting
50g strong wholemeal bread flour
325ml lukewarm water (22-23°C)
0.5g fast-action (easy-blend) dried yeast
13g fine pink Himalayan salt
extra virgin olive oil, for drizzling

In a bowl, mix the two types of flour together using a spoon, then sift the flour into another bowl to remove any lumps. In a separate bowl, combine the lukewarm water and yeast, stirring them together using a whisk. Add 325g of the flour and whisk the ingredients together until the mixture becomes smooth like a cream.

Add the salt to the remaining flour and mix together with a spoon, then slowly add this to the creamy flour mixture whilst whisking (2).

Once the dough becomes more solid, gently knead it inside the bowl using your knuckles, palms and fingers. With your left hand, spin the bowl anti-clockwise whilst folding the dough in half using your right hand. Repeat until the ingredients have combined (3).

Remove the dough from the bowl and knead it using both hands. Fold the dough in half and then stretch it. Repeat for a few minutes, until the dough becomes uniform and all the flour is combined into the dough (4).

Shape the dough into a ball, then cover it with the bowl. Leave it to rest for 10 minutes, so the flour can absorb the water, making it easier to knead the dough later. After 10 minutes, sprinkle a little flour onto the work surface, then remove the bowl and gently knead the dough using your fingertips and palms. Fold the dough in half and stretch it for a few minutes, until it becomes smooth and dry. Shape the dough into a ball, then cover it with the bowl and leave it to rest for 15 minutes (5).

Sprinkle a little flour onto the work surface, then remove the bowl and gently flatten the dough into a rectangle using your fingertips (6).

Pick up one side of the dough and fold it one-third of the way over the rest of the dough, then pick up the opposite side of the dough and gently stretch it over the first fold (7). Grab the top edge of the rectangle and fold it one-third of the way towards you, then grab the bottom edge of the dough and stretch it over the other folds. Now you will have a square (8).

Turn the square over and make the dough into a ball shape as shown (9 and 10). Pour a drizzle of olive oil into the bowl and spread it evenly on the sides using your hands. Place the dough into the bowl and cover it with clingfilm or a damp tea towel. Leave the dough to rest at an ambient (room) temperature of 20-23°C for 4 hours.

Once the dough is rested, remove it from the bowl, then place it on a floured surface. Divide the dough into four pieces of 200g each. Take one piece of dough at a time and flatten it using your fingertips, then grab each corner of the dough and fold it towards the centre, one by one, forming a little money pouch (11 and 12). Turn the dough ball over and gently apply a little pressure on it with a slightly cupped hand. Roll the ball around under your palm a few times, until the folds have been incorporated and have disappeared.

Place the dough balls on a tray (use a tray with raised sides about 4-5cm high) and cover it with clingfilm or a damp tea towel. Leave the dough balls to mature at an ambient temperature of 20-23°C for 4 hours. Once matured, use or store the dough balls as required.

SOURDOUGH STARTER

As the old adage goes, good things come to those who wait, and for those who have the time and patience, we'd always recommend creating your own sourdough starter for the perfect pizza dough every single time. Every bona fide *pizzaiolo* from Naples and beyond will be found using only natural sourdough for their pizzas.

What is sourdough?

At its core, sourdough is just flour, water and a little bit of nature's magic. By combining flour and water, and allowing it to react with the air, we can breed specific microorganisms within the dough that produce yeast and lactic acid – the component that gives sourdough its distinctive taste. This fermentation process is similar to how we'd make yogurt or wine.

Creating your unique starter

The goal here is to create a 'sourdough starter' or a 'mother', which is effectively a colony of bacteria numbering in the billions that can be added to future dough, taking the place of yeast. The good news is that once you've created your starter, a world of sourdough is unlocked and future dough will be quick and easy to make. All you need for future pizzas is flour, water and a little bit of your starter.

Your starter will be unique to you, with a ratio of bacteria within it that's a little different to every other sourdough starter in the world. This is why Italian families and pizzerias maintain their sourdough starters for decades, with some dating back over a century. All it needs is a little nurturing to keep the starter 'alive' and it'll be yours forever. See page 18 to learn how to care for your starter and keep it fed.

MAKES 360G STARTER

540g strong white bread flour
60g strong wholemeal bread flour
lukewarm water (ideally use bottled mineral water, heated to around 22-23°C)

Combine both flours together in an airtight container and set aside. You'll be using some of this flour every day, so keep it stored somewhere safe.

Combine 120g of the flour with 120ml lukewarm water in a large glass or plastic container (1 and 2). You'll be adding to this container every day, so ensure it's big enough to accommodate this. Stir vigorously (3), then cover with a breathable lid such as muslin cloth or a tea towel (4). Leave this in a warm place (but not too hot) around 20-23°C. For example, keep it near a radiator but not sitting on one.

After approximately 48 hours, stir the mixture and discard 120g of it. Add 120g flour and 120ml lukewarm water to the remaining mixture and combine, before covering again. As before, leave the mixture to rest in a warm place for 48 hours.

Repeat this step 3 times over the next 6 days. Look out for bubbling on the surface of the sourdough as this is an indication that the mixture is generating the bacteria that makes it so vital for making pizza.

From day 7, repeat the same process as above, but this time leave the mixture to rest for just 24 hours. Over the next few days, your starter should be doubling in size within 3 or 4 hours. The starter is now ready and can be used for making pizza.

Keeping your starter alive

Once you've prepared your sourdough starter, you'll need to keep it fed. This is a bit like feeding a living organism (although technically it consists of billions upon billions of living organisms). You'll need to feed it regularly just to keep it fresh, but you will also need to feed it before using it.

Fortunately, feeding is extremely simple! Here, we'll take you through how to keep your sourdough starter alive, and feeding it in preparation for use in pizza dough.

1. Ensure your starter is kept in the fridge at all times after it has developed. This keeps the bacteria from becoming overactive and lowers the risk of your sourdough going off. You'll need to feed it once every 4 days (approximately).

2. It likes to be fed on the same flour used to create it, so try to get the same flour brand repeatedly. If you used a flour blend, be sure to mix this to the same ratio. For feeding, your sourdough starter will need the equivalent to $1/3$ of its weight in flour and $1/3$ in water. For example, if you're aiming for a 300g sourdough starter, the easiest way to achieve this is to take 100g from your starter and mix it with 100g flour and 100g water.

3. Because the sourdough will 'adopt' the new flour and water mix, it'll continue to grow. As such, you'll need to remove some of the excess sourdough that's already in the starter to prevent the sourdough starter from growing too large. (You could always make some pizza with the spare you've separated, or even gift it to a pizza-loving friend).

4. That's it, your sourdough starter is fed! You'll need to do this again in about 4 days.

You can now decide whether to use some of it for baking your pizza or to keep it stored in the fridge.

If you decide to make pizza, remember to leave the amount of sourdough you are planning to use at room temperature (20-23°C) for at least 3-4 hours to allow the fermentation process to start.

Once the fermentation has started, the sourdough that you're using for baking is ready to be incorporated into your dough recipe, whilst your starter can continue to sit in the fridge.

For those making pizzas regularly, we recommend maintaining a starter that's at least 100-150g in weight (after feeding) at any time. This will give you the flexibility to make a pizza as and when you feel like it, simply by separating the starter into two portions of 50-75g. You will use half for the pizzas, and feed the other half as instructed opposite in order to maintain the starter.

If you aren't making pizzas regularly, then you can maintain a small starter (50-70g, after feeding, would be ideal).

It's better to maintain and feed a small starter if you don't use it regularly, as it wastes less flour and is less costly.

How to make dough with your sourdough starter

You can use this sourdough starter in our wholemeal dough recipe on pages 12-15 in place of dried yeast.

The ingredients will change as follows:
425g strong white bread flour, plus extra for dusting
50g strong wholemeal bread flour
300ml lukewarm water (22-23°C)
50g sourdough starter
13g fine pink Himalayan salt
extra virgin olive oil, for drizzling

All you need to do is follow our wholemeal dough recipe, mixing the sourdough starter with the water (5, 6 and 7) instead of the dried yeast before combining with the flour (8 and 9).

Dough made with sourdough starter can take a bit longer to ferment, especially in the winter when the temperature is lower, so it might take a little bit longer to achieve the final result. Try to prove your dough in a warm place, at around 22-23°C.

The end result of your dough will all depend on how healthy your sourdough starter is. It's like having a little pet - it will need your attention day by day.

GLUTEN-FREE DOUGH

We may be known for our Plant Pioneer innovations at Purezza, but we've put just as much work into our gluten-free offering.

A huge part of this was nailing the perfect gluten-free pizza base. One that we could serve with pride to anyone who was avoiding gluten. Most gluten-free pizza bases contain egg, which makes them non-vegan. This recipe was the result of numerous experiments, and in the end we cracked it – a gluten-free base that we truly think is indistinguishable from sourdough.

The first step is to create a gluten-free flour blend. You can make plenty of this and store it in a cool, dry place. The different flours react with one another in different ways, meaning you get a blend of tastes and textures that ultimately rival the best of sourdoughs.

The second step in the process is to create the pizzas. Once you have the flour blend ready, it's not all that dissimilar to making traditional dough, and just involves adding other components that will ensure the dough cooks and rises to perfection.

If you're cooking this for yourself, then enjoy! If you're cooking for someone else, just remember to avoid potential cross-contamination.

MAKES 700G

FOR THE GLUTEN-FREE FLOUR BLEND
310g rice flour
160g buckwheat flour
110g cornflour
120g potato starch
1¼ teaspoons xanthan gum

Sift together all the flours, potato starch and xanthan gum, then pour the mixture into an airtight glass jar or suitable container and shake vigorously. Cover with the lid and store in a cool, dry place. Before each use, shake and mix the flour blend well in the jar or container.

MAKES ENOUGH DOUGH FOR 4 PIZZAS

FOR THE PIZZAS

700g gluten-free flour blend
  (see page 19)
1.75g fast-action (easy-blend) dried
  yeast (or use 3.5g fresh yeast)
1 tablespoon soft brown sugar
530ml lukewarm water (22-23°C)
19g fine pink Himalayan salt
40ml extra virgin olive oil (for the mix),
  plus extra for greasing

Sift the flour blend into a bowl to remove any lumps (1). Add the yeast and sugar and mix together with a spatula (if you are using fresh yeast, crumble it with the flour making really small pieces)(2).

Add two-thirds of the lukewarm water and mix vigorously with a spatula, trying to combine all the flour with the water and avoiding any lumps (3). When the dough looks compact, dissolve the salt in the remaining water (4), then pour it into the bowl and keep mixing with the spatula. With your left hand, spin the bowl anti-clockwise, with the spatula in your right hand, folding the dough until you have a single and consistent ball (5).

At this point, add the olive oil, a little at a time, and keep mixing with the spatula until all of the oil is added and the dough has absorbed it all (6). Remove the dough from the bowl and lay it on a smooth, oiled surface. Helped by a dough scraper and having some oil on your hands, shape the dough into a smooth, round ball (7) and put it back into an oiled bowl. Cover with clingfilm or a damp tea towel and leave it to rest at an ambient temperature of 20-23°C for 1 hour (8).

Once rested, flip the dough onto a smooth surface and, using a dough scraper, divide it into four equal parts. On a separate surface, lay four sheets of clingfilm, each at least 30 x 30cm, one next to the other (this is for wrapping your dough balls).

Ensure that you put some oil on your hands to avoid the dough sticking to them. Take each piece of dough, one by one, and use your hands to shape it into a smooth ball. Put each ball in the centre of a clingfilm sheet and wrap, covering it completely with the clingfilm (9). Store the dough balls, separated from one another, in a large tray.

Keep them at an ambient temperature of 20-23°C for 2-3 hours before using, or put them in the fridge and use within 6 hours. Alternatively, you can freeze them straight away if you want to use them in the future (they can be frozen for up to 4 weeks). Remember to remove them from the freezer and defrost at room temperature for at least 8 hours before use.

CHAPTER 2

SAUCES

Our sauces are designed to be highly adaptable. We list them here as key components for the forthcoming chapter on pizzas. We have everything from the classics, such as Passata and Marinara sauces, to unique inventions. You haven't truly experienced how good pizza can be until you've tried a Christmas-inspired Red Cabbage Sauce as a base, or the refreshing springtime Pea or Asparagus sauces.

These sauces work just as well in other classic Italian dishes. Pasta and risotto are both enriched by their inclusion. We recommend making a larger batch size than you think you'll need for a pizza, and trying the remainder in one of your other Italian culinary expeditions.

SAN MARZANO PLUM TOMATO AND BASIL 'PASSATA' SAUCE

- PASSATA -

Long and skinny, San Marzano plum tomatoes are the superior variety of tomato for making pizza. They are specifically cultivated to have a high ratio of tomato flesh, compared to juice and seeds, making them easy to preserve. This also gives more actual tomato for turning into fantastic sauce.

Although the San Marzano variety can be grown anywhere, the official San Marzano tomatoes must come from the region around San Marzano, Italy, an area with rich volcanic soil at the base of Mount Vesuvius, which gives them a sweet flavour and low acidity content. To ensure the tomatoes you are buying are truly San Marzano tomatoes, check for the DOP designation on the label.

**MAKES 200ML
(ENOUGH FOR 4 PIZZAS)**

500g San Marzano plum tomatoes
a handful of basil leaves
½ teaspoon fine pink Himalayan salt

Wash the tomatoes, place them in a heatproof bowl, cover with boiling water and leave for 2–3 minutes, then drain them using a colander.

Pass the tomatoes through a food mill (or use a food processor and sieve) and collect the pulp in a bowl. Wash the basil leaves, discard the stalks and finely chop the leaves, then add to the pulp along with the salt and stir to mix.

Use the sauce immediately, or transfer it to an airtight container and store in the fridge for up to 3 days.

Pictured on page 37, number 1.

REGULAR TOMATO SAUCE

A good alternative to San Marzano fresh tomatoes are peeled canned tomatoes, which are the key for preparing a quick and tasty tomato sauce for your pizza. We recommend using peeled tomatoes because they are of a better quality than pre-chopped tomatoes. You can add extra flavour by mixing the sauce with basil leaves.

**MAKES 250ML
(ENOUGH FOR 4 PIZZAS)**

240g canned whole peeled plum tomatoes
a few basil leaves
a pinch of fine pink Himalayan salt

In a large bowl, crush the tomatoes by squeezing them using your hands. Wash the basil leaves, discard the stalks and finely chop the leaves, then add to the tomato pulp along with the salt and stir to mix.

Use the sauce immediately, or transfer it to an airtight container and store in the fridge for up to 3 days.

Pictured on page 36, number 2.

MARINARA SAUCE

A truly traditional Italian classic. One of the simplest sauces to prepare, and yet we still find ourselves coming back to this one again and again. It's that good. Marinara sauce is not dissimilar to our passata, but the additions of a small amount of onion, some garlic and some oregano lead to subtle new flavours coming to the fore.

MAKES ENOUGH SAUCE FOR 4 PIZZAS

1 tablespoon extra virgin olive oil
¼ yellow onion, finely chopped
1 garlic clove, crushed or minced
400g canned whole peeled plum
   tomatoes, crushed by hand
1 teaspoon dried oregano
a few basil leaves
a pinch of fine pink Himalayan salt
a pinch of freshly ground black pepper

Heat the olive oil in a large saucepan over a low heat for 30 seconds. Add the onion and garlic and soften them for 1 minute. Add the tomatoes, oregano and basil.

Continue to cook over a medium heat for approximately 20 minutes, maintaining a steady simmer and stirring occasionally.

By this time, the sauce should have reduced slightly and be thicker, so you can then take it off the heat. Season the sauce with the salt and black pepper.

Use the sauce immediately, or transfer it to an airtight container and store in the fridge for up to 3 days.

Pictured on page 36, number 3.

SUN-DRIED TOMATO PESTO SAUCE

At Purezza, we enjoy offering different alternatives to the traditional tomato sauce. This spreadable sun-dried tomato pesto sauce adds a very delicate and creamy texture to any pizza that has fresh and light toppings. We recommend using this sauce with spring or summer vegetables.

MAKES ENOUGH SAUCE FOR 4 PIZZAS

160g sun-dried tomatoes in oil
3 basil leaves
330ml Regular Tomato Sauce (see page 25)
15g walnuts
1½ tablespoons pine nuts
1 teaspoon nutritional yeast
a pinch of fine pink Himalayan salt

Add the sun-dried tomatoes, basil and tomato sauce to a bowl and blend them together using a handheld blender (or use a blender or food processor).

Once the mixture is smooth, add the walnuts, pine nuts, nutritional yeast and salt, then blend again until the pesto becomes creamy.

Use the sauce immediately, or transfer it to an airtight container and store in the fridge for up to 3 days.

Pictured on page 37, number 4.

BUTTERNUT SQUASH SAUCE

Butternut squash sauce is a good alternative to tomato sauce. With its sweet, nutty taste, similar to that of a pumpkin, and its creamy texture, it makes a perfect base for a winter pizza! It is also a good source of fibre, vitamin C, magnesium, potassium and vitamin A.

MAKES ENOUGH SAUCE FOR 4 PIZZAS

1 tablespoon extra virgin olive oil
½ shallot, finely chopped
1 butternut squash (about 300g total weight), peeled, deseeded and cut into large cubes
1 tablespoon vegan white wine
1 teaspoon fine pink Himalayan salt
350ml rice milk (or any other plant-based milk, but avoid coconut milk)
a pinch of freshly ground black pepper

Heat the olive oil in a saucepan over a low heat for 30 seconds, add the shallot and let it soften for 1 minute.

Add the butternut squash cubes and cook for 1 minute, then add the wine and stir. Cook over a medium heat for 5 minutes, adding 240ml of water to prevent the squash from burning.

Once the water has reduced, add the salt and 240ml of the rice milk. Stir and cook for 4–5 minutes until the butternut squash becomes soft, then transfer it to a heatproof bowl (or food processor).

Add the remaining rice milk and blend, using a handheld blender (or food processor) until the mixture becomes creamy. Add the black pepper and mix it again.

Use the sauce immediately, or transfer it to an airtight container and store in the fridge for up to 3 days.

Pictured on page 37, number 5.

YELLOW CHERRY TOMATO SAUCE

Yellow cherry tomatoes make for an excellent alternative to classic tomato sauce using San Marzano tomatoes. Yellow cherry tomatoes pack their own distinctive flavour profile, primarily because they have comparably low acidity, meaning you get sweeter flavour notes to your pizzas. Their vibrant colour and fresh, sweet flavour make them a great addition to summer pizzas. Buy a few extra and make a delicious side salad to go with your pizza.

MAKES ENOUGH SAUCE FOR 4 PIZZAS

1kg yellow cherry tomatoes, halved
2 tablespoons extra virgin olive oil
1 teaspoon fine pink Himalayan salt

Place the tomatoes in a large saucepan, and cook for 20 minutes over a low heat, stirring occasionally. Take the pan off the heat and allow the tomatoes to cool for an hour.

Tip the tomatoes into a sieve or a food mill and press them to separate the pulp from the skin and seeds. Pour the pulp into a saucepan, add the olive oil and salt, and cook over a low heat, stirring occasionally, until the sauce is reduced, about 5 minutes.

Use the sauce immediately, or transfer it to an airtight container and store in the fridge for up to 3 days.

Pictured on page 36, number 6.

PEA SAUCE

We crafted this sauce for a Valentine's special at Purezza called Peas & Love. It was such a huge hit throughout the entire month of February that we decided to give away the recipe for our eponymous pea sauce in this book. This sauce makes for a creamy combo of sweet and savoury notes. Peas are high in protein and fibre, too, making this a very filling and healthy addition to your pizza. Some people might be put off by the green-looking base, but hey, why not give peas a chance?

MAKES ENOUGH SAUCE FOR 4 PIZZAS

1 tablespoon extra virgin olive oil
½ shallot, thinly sliced
200g frozen green peas
2 tablespoons vegan white wine
½ teaspoon fine pink Himalayan salt
a pinch of crushed dried chillies
160ml rice milk (or any other plant-
    based milk, but avoid coconut milk)
a pinch of freshly ground black pepper

Heat the olive oil in a saucepan over a low heat for 30 seconds, then add the shallot and soften for 1 minute. Stir in the peas and cook for 1 minute.

Increase the heat to medium, then add the wine and cook the peas for a couple of minutes or so until they turn soft. Add the salt and crushed chillies and stir for a few seconds. Take the pan off the heat and allow the mixture to cool.

Once cooled, transfer the pea mixture to a blender (or use a handheld blender or food processor), along with the rice milk, and blend together, adding the black pepper after the initial blending. Continue to blend until smooth.

Use the sauce immediately, or transfer it to an airtight container and store in the fridge for up to 3 days.

Pictured on page 36, number 7.

ASPARAGUS SAUCE

Asparagus has one of the most unique flavours when it comes to green vegetables. It's both fresh and mild, whilst also offering deep earthy notes. Simultaneously distinctive and blending well with the flavours you cook it with, the asparagus sings in this recipe, getting just a little boost from garlic and lemon. Much of this recipe's final flavour will be dependent on the quality of asparagus you buy. Fresh, organic asparagus bought at the height of its season (roughly late April to mid-June in the UK) will make a world of difference.

MAKES ENOUGH SAUCE FOR 4 PIZZAS

1 tablespoon extra virgin olive oil
1 garlic clove, finely chopped
200g fresh asparagus, woody stalks trimmed, spears cut into 2-3cm lengths
1½ tablespoons vegan white wine
½ teaspoon fine pink Himalayan salt
juice of ½ lemon
80ml rice milk (or any other plant-based milk, but avoid coconut milk)
a pinch of freshly ground black pepper

Heat the olive oil in a saucepan over a medium heat for 30 seconds, then add the garlic. Add the asparagus and stir for 1 minute, then stir in the wine. Let the asparagus cook for 5 minutes, slowly adding 50ml of water to prevent the asparagus from burning. Once the water has reduced, add the salt and lemon juice. Take the pan off the heat and allow the mixture to cool.

Once cooled, transfer the asparagus mixture to a blender (or use a handheld blender or food processor) along with the rice milk and blend together, adding the black pepper after the initial blending. Continue to blend until smooth.

The sauce should be smooth enough to use on pizzas, but not too thick, either. If it's too thick, it can end up burning when cooking the pizzas, so add a little water to loosen it, if necessary.

Use the sauce immediately, or transfer it to an airtight container and store in the fridge for up to 3 days.

Pictured on page 37, number 8.

CHICKPEA AND LEMON SAUCE

This encapsulates summer for us. A zingy, zesty sauce that's aromatic with the fresh flavours of lemon and rosemary. It's a key component in one of our favourite midsummer pizzas, featured later in the book (page 106), where we combine it with earthy mushrooms and salty pancetta, but we love this sauce so much that it often finds its way into our pasta dishes, too. It's easy to make and packed with healthy ingredients, including plant-powered protein from the chickpeas, and that all-important vitamin C from the lemon juice.

MAKES ENOUGH SAUCE FOR 4 PIZZAS

1 tablespoon extra virgin olive oil
½ shallot, thinly sliced
190g (drained weight) canned or cooked chickpeas, rinsed and drained (see Tip)
½ teaspoon fine pink Himalayan salt
½ sprig of rosemary
100ml rice milk (or any other plant-based milk, but avoid coconut milk)
juice of ½ lemon
a pinch of freshly ground black pepper

Heat the olive oil in a saucepan over a low heat for 30 seconds, then add the shallot and sweat for 1 minute. Stir in the chickpeas and soften for 1 minute. Add the salt and rosemary and stir for 1 minute. Take the pan off the heat, remove the rosemary sprig and allow the mixture to cool.

Once cooled, transfer the chickpea mixture to a blender (or use a handheld blender or food processor) along with the rice milk and lemon juice, and blend together, adding the black pepper after the initial blending. Continue to blend until smooth.

The sauce should be smooth enough to use on pizzas, but not too thick, either. If it's too thick, it can end up burning when cooking the pizzas, so add a little water to loosen it, if necessary.

Use the sauce immediately, or transfer it to an airtight container and store in the fridge for up to 3 days.

Pictured on page 36, number 9.

Tip If using canned chickpeas, drain the liquid into a separate container and save it for another recipe, such as our Garlic Mayonnaise (see page 74) or Tiramisù (see page 134).

RED CABBAGE SAUCE

This gorgeously creamy, smooth sauce makes for a pizza that'll impress on both a visual and a taste level. Visually this sauce gives your pizza base a beautiful pink coating that looks quite unlike anything else. The flavour is rich with a gentle sweet note from the red cabbage. What's more, red cabbage is packed with health benefits including the anti-ageing powerhouse, anthocyanin, which gives it its distinctive colour.

It regularly makes an appearance around Christmas for us in the Purezza restaurants, where we typically use it as the sauce for a festive pizza for our specials menu. It pairs particularly well with parsnips, as in a recipe you'll find later in this book. Truthfully though, we'd happily eat it all year round...

MAKES ENOUGH SAUCE FOR 4 PIZZAS

1 tablespoon extra virgin olive oil
½ shallot, finely chopped
150g red cabbage, chopped
1 tablespoon vegan white wine
200ml rice milk
½ teaspoon fine pink Himalayan salt
a pinch of freshly ground black pepper

Heat the olive oil in a saucepan over a low heat for 30 seconds, then add the shallot and sweat for 1 minute. Stir in the red cabbage and soften for 1 minute. Add the wine and stir, then allow the red cabbage to cook over a medium heat for 8 minutes until it becomes soft, stirring occasionally.

Add 90ml of the milk and the salt, and allow the mixture to cook for a further 8 minutes until the cabbage becomes very soft, and the milk is reduced, stirring occasionally. Take the pan off the heat and allow the mixture to cool.

Once cooled, transfer the cabbage mixture to a blender (or use a handheld blender or food processor), along with the remaining milk and blend until smooth. Finally, stir in the black pepper.

Use the sauce immediately, or transfer it to an airtight container and store in the fridge for up to 3 days.

Pictured on page 36, number 10.

CHEESES

This is where the Plant Pioneer magic truly begins. Cheese, glorious cheese, but made with plants alone. These recipes are the result of years of research and innovation. We've got the works here, from your classic mozzarella to smooth and creamy spreadable cheese sauce, from grated Parmesan to sharp and biting Gorgonzola, from the mild and gentle ricotta to the strong, salty pecorino. This chapter will open up a whole culinary world for you to explore, and whilst these cheeses have been created with pizza in mind, please feel free to enjoy any of these with dishes of your choosing.

CASHEW MOZZARELLA

Sometimes it can be challenging to find a good plant-based mozzarella that is easy to prepare without having to go on a hunt for numerous exotic ingredients. Here, we use only seven readily available ingredients!

At our restaurants, we use a more complex recipe for producing our unique mozzarella, which is completely allergen-free. For the purposes of this book, we recommend a simple and quick, cashew-based mozzarella recipe that can be prepared in a few minutes at home. Where most recipes will call for soaked nuts, we use blanched nuts so you can prepare the cheese and enjoy it the same day.

MAKES 280G

80g blanched unsalted cashew nuts
1 teaspoon fine pink Himalayan salt
100ml almond milk (with at least 5% almond content)
1 tablespoon apple cider vinegar
2 tablespoons nutritional yeast
½ tablespoon tapioca
100ml flavourless coconut oil

Add all the ingredients to a high-speed blender and blend them together until smooth and combined, scraping down the sides once or twice, if necessary. Check the texture - it should be extremely smooth with no lumps.

Place a layer of clingfilm inside a shallow container and pour the mixture in. Place the container in the fridge for at least 1 hour to set and become firm. Once set, it is ready to use.

The mozzarella will keep in an airtight container in the fridge for up to 3 days. To use, slice the mozzarella and scatter over your chosen pizza.

Pictured on page 42, number 1.

GRATED NUT PARMESAN

Parmesan is one of Italy's most widely loved cheeses, but its traditional recipe isn't even vegetarian, let alone vegan. Fortunately, its complex, nutty flavour profile isn't actually hard to replicate.

This versatile cheese adds an extra punch of flavour to pasta, lasagne and any pizza you fancy sprinkling it over.

MAKES 250G

50g blanched unsalted almonds
50g blanched unsalted cashew nuts
10g nutritional yeast
½ teaspoon fine pink Himalayan salt

Add all the ingredients to a high-speed blender. Using the pulse setting, pulse the mixture two or three times to create a dusted Parmesan effect. Avoid over-blending as this will create a paste.

Tip the Parmesan into a bowl and use as required, dusting it over your chosen pizza or pasta. It will keep in an airtight container for 3 days. Pictured on page 42, number 2.

ALMOND GORGONZOLA CHEESE

Gorgonzola cheese originates from the town of Gorgonzola, a few miles away from Milan. Its main characteristics are the green-blue spots, the sharp, salty and nutty taste, and the crumbly, soft texture. Generally it takes around 4 months to produce this cheese, but here it is, a vegan recipe, which takes only 4 minutes to prepare and around 30 minutes to set!

MAKES 200G

100g blanched unsalted almonds
100ml flavourless coconut oil
juice of ½ lemon
½ teaspoon fine pink Himalayan salt
1 garlic clove, peeled
75ml almond milk (with at least 5% almond content)
1 tablespoon apple cider vinegar
a sprinkle of spirulina powder

Add all the ingredients, except the spirulina, to a high-speed blender and blend together until smooth, about 2 minutes, scraping down the sides if necessary.

Place a layer of clingfilm inside a shallow container and pour in the mixture. Sprinkle the spirulina across the mixture, then firmly fold (not stir) the mixture in on itself several times to create a marbled effect.

Place the container in the fridge for at least 30 minutes to set. Once set, use as required, placing over your chosen pizza. The cheese will keep in an airtight container in the fridge for up to 3 days. Pictured on page 43, number 3.

CASHEW AND WALNUT PECORINO

After Parmesan, this is arguably the second most well-known hard cheese in Italy. Pecorino uses sheep's milk in its production, giving it a flavour profile that's sharper and saltier than other cheeses.

This blend of natural ingredients provides the same flavours as pecorino, and by using walnuts as the core ingredient for this cheese, we get a deeper and richer overall flavour profile, more akin to traditional pecorino cheese.

MAKES 250G

180g blanched unsalted cashew nuts
45g walnuts
6 tablespoons flavourless coconut oil
2 tablespoons freshly squeezed lemon juice
1½ tablespoons apple cider vinegar
2 tablespoons nutritional yeast
1 garlic clove, peeled
½ teaspoon fine pink Himalayan salt

Add the cashews and walnuts to a high-speed blender and whizz until lightly textured (but not completely smooth). Transfer this mixture to a bowl.

Add all the remaining ingredients to the blender and whizz together until smooth.

Pour the blended ingredients into the bowl with the nuts and mix them together using your hands until all the ingredients have combined.

Pour the mixture into an airtight container and leave it to set in the fridge overnight. Once rested, use as required, crumbling over your chosen pizza.

The pecorino will keep in an airtight container in the fridge for up to 3 days.

Pictured on page 43, number 4.

ALMOND RICOTTA

Ricotta production in Italy dates back to the Bronze Age. With such heritage and history, we had to apply the Plant Pioneers philosophy to it and create a modern version with plant-based ingredients. This is simple to make, using almonds as the core ingredient. It's packed with protein, so that you can feel good about putting some of this cheese onto, well, everything you eat.

MAKES ENOUGH FOR 4 PIZZAS

125g blanched unsalted almonds
juice of ½ lemon
½ teaspoon fine pink Himalayan salt
¾ teaspoon apple cider vinegar
1 tablespoon nutritional yeast
¼ garlic clove, peeled
100ml almond milk (with at least 5% almond content)

Add all the ingredients to a high-speed blender and blend together to mix, then continue to blend for about a further minute until it creates a thick, lumpy mixture (which can be directly applied to pizzas), scraping down the sides once or twice, if necessary. You don't want it to be completely smooth.

Tip the ricotta into a bowl and use as required, spreading or dolloping it onto your chosen pizza using a tablespoon or piping bag and nozzle. It will keep in an airtight container in the fridge for up to 3 days. Pictured on page 43, number 6.

SPREADABLE CHEESE

- WITH CAPERS AND CHIVES -

A gorgeously creamy cheese that will have your friends staring at you in disbelief when you rustle it up and serve it to them, be it on a pizza, in pasta or just as a side with some crusty bread. We use nutritional yeast to give a cheesy flavour, pairing it with lemon juice, capers, chives and salt. This sauce is incredibly versatile. In fact, it becomes difficult to resist slathering it on pretty much everything.

MAKES ENOUGH FOR 4 PIZZAS

250g blanched unsalted cashew nuts
2 tablespoons nutritional yeast
juice of 1 lemon
1 tablespoon capers, drained
½ teaspoon fine pink Himalayan salt
1 tablespoon chopped chives

Place the cashews in a large bowl and cover with cold water. Cover the bowl with clingfilm and leave to soak overnight or for at least 4 hours at room temperature.

Drain and rinse the cashews, then add them to a high-speed blender, along with the nutritional yeast, lemon juice, capers, salt and 1 tablespoon of water. Whizz until very smooth, about 5 minutes. You may need to occasionally stop and scrape the sides down with a spatula. Transfer the cashew cheese to a dish or bowl and stir through the chives. Cover with clingfilm and place in the fridge for 1 hour to firm up a little before use, spreading it over your chosen pizza. The cheese sauce will keep, covered, in the fridge for up to 3 days. Pictured on page 42, number 5.

CASHEW BUFFALO MOZZARELLA

Buffalo mozzarella, or *fior di latte* mozzarella, is the gold standard in Italian cheese. This ingenious recipe will have you crafting beautiful rounded balls of buffalo mozzarella, but leaving the buffaloes well alone.

This one is a really fun recipe to make. Using thermal shock, you'll craft a mixture and set it suddenly in ice-cold water. A few minutes of chilling the ingredients and you'll have a ball of mozzarella that can be used just like traditional buffalo mozzarella. Try it in a traditional Italian salad before moving on to the main event, where you can enjoy it sliced over a pizza.

MAKES ENOUGH FOR 4 PIZZAS

ice cubes (for chilling the water)
100g blanched unsalted cashew nuts
1 teaspoon fine pink Himalayan salt
200ml almond milk (with at least
    5% almond content)
½ tablespoon apple cider vinegar
1½ tablespoons nutritional yeast
3 tablespoons tapioca

Fill a large bowl with cold water and ice, and set it to one side.

Add all the remaining ingredients to a high-speed blender and blend them together on full speed until smooth and combined, scraping down the sides once or twice, if necessary.

Transfer the mixture to a saucepan and cook over a medium heat for about 2 minutes, stirring, until the mixture becomes thicker and clumps together. Remove the pan from the heat.

Using a large spoon, scoop out balls of the cheese mixture and place them into the bowl of iced water. This will rapidly cool the balls, firming them up. Leave in the iced water for about 5 minutes to continue to firm up. They should have a smooth and rubbery texture when they are ready. You can then remove the mozzarella balls from the water using a slotted spoon, and slice them up for recipes.

Store any leftover mozzarella balls in an airtight container in the fridge for up to 3 days.

TOPPINGS

This range of toppings has been designed to marry with the sauces and cheeses you'll be using in the upcoming pizza recipes. But don't let that stop you from making these without any particular pizza in mind. They work fantastically well as side dishes to be served alongside your mains during dinner. If we're hosting a pizza evening, we typically make a few extra sides or salads that use these toppings as core components.

MELANZANE 'A FUNGHETTO'

Perhaps one of the most confusingly named dishes in Italian culinary history, *melanzane a funghetto* roughly translates as 'mushroom-style aubergine'. There's not a hint of mushroom in this one, but instead the 'mushroom-style' alludes to the way the dish is cooked. This recipe will have you frying and sautéing aubergines in a similar manner to how you would mushrooms, ensuring any liquid is completely removed and the aubergines are given a gentle golden browning.

This highly adaptable dish is great to have on hand all year round. In winter, it acts like a warm and hearty stew, whilst in summer you can cool it and use it as a side or antipasti. Tastes great on pizza, tastes great on pasta... honestly, it tastes great with everything!

MAKES ENOUGH FOR 4 PIZZAS

2 medium aubergines
fine pink Himalayan salt, for sprinkling
150ml extra virgin olive oil, plus extra
  for frying
2 garlic cloves, finely chopped
120g large tomatoes, cut into 1cm pieces
a few basil leaves, chopped or torn
  into small pieces

Cut the aubergines into 1cm cubes, putting the cubes into a colander as you go and sprinkling them with plenty of salt. The salt will help the aubergines to dry out, so once all the cubes are salted, leave them to sit (over a sink or bowl) for at least 30 minutes.

Take whole handfuls of the salted aubergine cubes, lay them on kitchen paper, then wrap them up in the paper and squeeze out any excess water from them. Drop the dried aubergines into a large bowl and repeat with the remaining aubergine cubes.

Heat the olive oil in a pan over a medium heat (this isn't like simulating deep-fat frying, but there should be an abundance of oil in the pan) until hot. Add the aubergine and fry until it begins to crisp and brown around the edges, turning occasionally. At this stage, the aubergine should be tender but still have a good structure. Lay the fried aubergine cubes out on a baking sheet lined with kitchen paper to absorb any excess oil.

Heat some olive oil in a separate large pan over a low heat and add in the garlic. After about 30 seconds, when the garlic is just beginning to give off its aroma, add the tomatoes and 5-6 chopped basil leaves and sauté over a very brisk heat, stirring often, until the tomatoes have reduced and begin to resemble a chunky sauce.

Carefully add the aubergine to the tomato mixture - the aubergine will be very tender at this point, so gently stir the mixtures together without damaging the aubergine. Finally, stir in a pinch of salt and a little extra chopped basil, and serve.

CARAMELISED ONIONS

Caramelised onions are one of the most versatile ingredients to use on pizzas. Their sweetness marries well with different sorts of toppings, especially the bitter ones. They balance perfectly with the distinctive flavour of radicchio rosso, chicory, cavolo nero and other green leafy vegetables.

MAKES ENOUGH FOR 4 PIZZAS

1 tablespoon sunflower oil
200g red onions, finely sliced
a pinch of fine pink Himalayan salt
2 tablespoons soft brown sugar
2 tablespoons balsamic vinegar

Heat the sunflower oil in a pan over a low heat. Add the red onions and salt and cook for 15 minutes, stirring occasionally. Once the onions are softened and become golden, stir in the sugar and vinegar.

Continue to cook the onions over a low heat for a further 5–6 minutes, until they become sticky and caramelised. Use as required.

AUBERGINE 'MEATBALLS'

The name might suggest otherwise, but meatballs are actually very easy to make vegan. That's because most of the flavours that you experience when eating them don't come from the meat itself, but rather from everything else they're crammed together with. By replacing the meat with mashed aubergine and breadcrumbs, we can pack these balls full of flavour from parsley and chilli flakes.

MAKES ENOUGH FOR 4 PIZZAS

¼ teaspoon fine pink Himalayan salt, plus extra for salting the water
2 medium aubergines
150g stale bread (or gluten-free stale bread)
a pinch of dried chilli flakes
a pinch of chopped parsley
70g rice flour
100g fresh breadcrumbs (or gluten-free breadcrumbs)
200ml sunflower oil

Begin by pouring 1 litre of water into a saucepan (use a large pan as you'll be adding plenty of aubergine to it!). Bring to the boil and add a little salt.

Meanwhile, peel the aubergines and cut them into 1cm cubes, then add these to the boiling water and simmer for 10 minutes.

Drain the aubergines, then lay the cubes out on a tray or similar, place a chopping board or baking tray over them with a few tins on top to weigh the board or tray down. Leave the aubergines to cool like this, so they become well drained.

Next, lightly soak the stale bread in water - place the bread in a shallow dish, cover with cold water and leave to soak for about 10 minutes. Ensure to squeeze it afterwards - it needs to be damp, but you want to remove any excess water.

Put the aubergines, soaked bread, chilli flakes and parsley into a blender and begin blending at a medium speed until combined. Add the rice flour (which will thicken the mixture up) and blend, then add the measured salt and blend to mix.

Once it is ready, form the mixture into meatballs (each about the size of a ping-pong ball - you should make about 25 in total), squeezing the mixture tightly in your hands to compact each one, then coat all the meatballs in breadcrumbs.

Heat the sunflower oil in a deep-fat fryer (or a large pan or wok) to a temperature of 180°C or until a cube of bread browns in 30 seconds. Deep-fry the meatballs in the hot oil (in batches) for about 2 minutes. Remove with a slotted spoon and drain on kitchen paper to remove the excess oil, then serve.

PARMIGIANA

This gorgeous aubergine parmigiana is our tried and tested recipe. We use it on our Parmigiana Pizza at Purezza – the pizza that won the National Pizza of the Year award in 2018. Like all good parmigiana recipes, we leave the aubergine buttery soft and marinated in rich flavours. This works as a recipe on its own, served with some of our Cashew Mozzarella layered over it, but is equally fantastic on a parmigiana pizza.

SERVES 4

500g aubergines
1 tablespoon fine pink Himalayan salt
50g rice flour
50ml sunflower oil
300ml Regular Tomato Sauce (see page 25)
120g Cashew Mozzarella (see page 40)
a few basil leaves, torn
50g nutritional yeast

Slice the aubergines about 5mm thick, putting the slices into a colander as you go, and sprinkling them with the salt (the salt will help the aubergines to dry out). When this is done, place the colander in the sink and place a heavy pan on top of the aubergines. Leave for about 30 minutes.

Preheat the oven to 180°C (gas mark 4).

Rinse the aubergine slices with fresh water to remove the excess salt, and then pat them dry with kitchen paper. Dip the aubergine slices into the rice flour, ensuring they are coated all over.

Heat the sunflower oil in a pan over a medium-high heat until hot. Add 3-4 aubergine slices at a time to the pan, and cook them for 1 minute on each side.

Remove the slices from the pan and drain on kitchen paper to remove the excess oil. Repeat until all the aubergine slices have been fried.

Take a deep oven dish and spread a layer of the tomato sauce on the base. Add the aubergine slices on top of this, then coat them in a further layer of the remaining tomato sauce. Place the cashew mozzarella in the gaps between the slices of aubergine. Scatter over the basil leaves and sprinkle the nutritional yeast over the top.

Bake in the oven for 40 minutes, at which point the parmigiana mixture should be browning on top and the aubergines should be soft, then serve.

FUNGHI TRIFOLATI

Funghi trifolati (or sautéd mushrooms in Italian) literally translates as 'truffled mushrooms'. They are so called because the thinly sliced and sautéd mushrooms are said to resemble truffles. This is, without a doubt, the most traditional way to cook mushrooms in Italy. High in vitamin D, selenium and fibre, *funghi trifolati* can be enjoyed on a pizza at any time of the year.

MAKES ENOUGH FOR 4 PIZZAS

2 tablespoons extra virgin olive oil
2 garlic cloves, finely chopped
300g mixed fresh mushrooms, thinly sliced
1 tablespoon vegan white wine
a handful of fresh parsley, roughly chopped
1 teaspoon fine pink Himalayan salt
a pinch of freshly ground black pepper

Put the olive oil and garlic in a pan and cook over a low heat for 30 seconds. Add the mushrooms and soften them for 10 minutes, periodically adding a dash of the white wine throughout this time.

Once the mushrooms have softened, add the parsley, salt and black pepper and stir for a few seconds. Use as required.

SMOKED BEETROOT CARPACCIO

Carpaccio is a Venetian dish, traditionally made using meats, such as beef or veal, or sometimes fish. We've opted for beautiful beetroot - a superfood that's loaded with nutrition, and brings an aesthetic vibrancy to any pizza you use it on, with its deep purple colouring. Looks amazing, tastes amazing!

MAKES ENOUGH FOR 4 PIZZAS

250g raw beetroots
1 tablespoon sunflower oil
½ tablespoon extra virgin olive oil
½ teaspoon apple cider vinegar
1 teaspoon smoked paprika
¼ teaspoon fine pink Himalayan salt

Preheat the oven to 180°C (gas mark 4) and line a baking tray with baking paper.

Peel the beetroots, then cut them into 2mm-thick slices. Combine all the remaining ingredients in a bowl, then add the beetroot slices to this mixture and toss gently until the slices are coated all over.

Lay out the sliced beetroot on the prepared baking tray in a single layer, drizzle over the marinade, and then cover with foil. Bake in the oven for 30 minutes, until they are cooked and softened. Remove from the oven and allow the beetroot slices to cool before serving as carpaccio.

ROASTED POTATOES

- WITH GARLIC AND ROSEMARY -

'Potatoes on pizza?' we hear you cry. But wait, don't knock this until you've tried it. In the restaurant, we've been serving up roast potatoes on pizza for several years with our long-term menu feature, the Couch Potato. In fact, *pizza con patate* is an Italian classic. This is comfort food at its very best.

MAKES ENOUGH FOR 4 PIZZAS

250g white potatoes, scrubbed
1 tablespoon extra virgin olive oil
1 garlic clove, finely chopped
1 sprig of rosemary
¼ teaspoon fine pink Himalayan salt
¼ teaspoon freshly ground black pepper

Preheat the oven to 180°C (gas mark 4) and line a baking tray with baking paper.

Slice the potatoes into 2mm-thick slices and place in a bowl of fresh, cold water to prevent any oxidation. Combine all the remaining ingredients in a separate bowl.

Drain the potato slices, pat them dry, then add the potatoes to the garlic/herb mixture and stir until coated all over. Lay out the potato slices on the prepared baking tray in a single layer, ensuring they don't overlap.

Bake in the oven for about 15 minutes, until the potatoes are cooked and start to turn golden brown. Discard the rosemary stalk. Use the potatoes as required.

STIR-FRIED CHICORY

- WITH CAPERS, GARLIC AND OLIVES -

Chicory is one of the healthiest foods in the world, packing abundant amounts of vitamins from A to K, and plenty of minerals. It's got great texture for pizza too. It sits somewhere between spinach and kale, offering a subtle flavour and gentle bite. By combining it with chilli, olives and capers, this makes for a great backdrop to more richly flavoured components. To give an authentic Italian twist to this topping, scarole or escarole can also be used.

MAKES ENOUGH FOR 4 PIZZAS

400g chicory (or scarole/escarole)
1½ tablespoons extra virgin olive oil
1 garlic clove, finely chopped
a pinch of dried chilli flakes
40g pitted Kalamata black olives,
    thinly sliced
5 capers, drained and rinsed
a pinch of fine pink Himalayan salt

Rinse the chicory thoroughly, as dirt can often sit within the leaves. Remove the leaves, then slice off the bottom parts where it pales to white.

Heat the olive oil in a large pan over a medium heat, add the garlic and chilli flakes and fry for 30 seconds. Add the still-wet chicory to the pan - if you can't fit it all in, let the first batch wilt a little before adding the rest.

Add the olives, capers and salt and sauté the mixture over a medium-high heat for 5 minutes. The chicory should be well wilted by this point, and much of the released water will have evaporated. Use as required. This will keep in an airtight container in the fridge for up to 3 days.

STIR-FRIED WILD BROCCOLI

A love letter to broccoli. Britain's favourite vegetable gets the Italian treatment (although, in case you didn't notice, the name 'broccoli' is of Italian origin). Varieties such as tenderstem broccoli are our favourite, as they emphasise use of the full plant rather than just the flowering tops, and the stem packs a satisfying crunch on pizza. This recipe is so incredibly simple, and yet will make you fall in love with broccoli again. If you can source *friarielli*, an Italian variety of broccoli from Naples, you can try this tasty alternative.

MAKES ENOUGH FOR 4 PIZZAS

400g wild broccoli, tenderstem broccoli or *friarielli*
3 tablespoons extra virgin olive oil
1 garlic clove, chopped
a pinch of dried chilli flakes
¼ teaspoon fine pink Himalayan salt

Rinse the broccoli thoroughly and remove the thick parts of the stems as well as any leaves.

Heat the olive oil in a frying pan over a medium heat, add the garlic and cook until it is golden, but do not burn it. Add the chilli flakes and the still-wet broccoli, cover the pan with the lid and cook for about 2–3 minutes.

Remove the lid and cook for a further 5 minutes, stirring occasionally. When the broccoli is tender, you can turn off the heat. Finally, add the salt and stir the mixture once more. Use as required. This will keep in an airtight container in the fridge for up to 3 days.

PAN-FRIED PEPPERS

- WITH GARLIC MARINADE -

An oh-so-simple recipe that'll turn peppers into your favourite vegetable. Some of the Mediterranean's punchiest flavours come together in this garlic marinade, which also contains white wine, black pepper and capers. The end result is peppers unlike any you've tasted before and that make a fantastic addition to any pizza.

MAKES ENOUGH FOR 4 PIZZAS

2 tablespoons extra virgin olive oil
3 garlic cloves, chopped
3 peppers (1 each of green, yellow and red), deseeded and sliced into long strips
1 tablespoon vegan white wine
5 capers, drained
¼ teaspoon fine pink Himalayan salt
a pinch of freshly ground black pepper

Heat the olive oil in a pan over a low heat for 30 seconds, then add the garlic and soften for 30 seconds. Add the mixed peppers to the pan and gently cook them for 10 minutes, stirring occasionally, adding the white wine partway through this period.

Add the capers, salt and black pepper to the peppers and stir everything together.

Finally, add 4 tablespoons of water and cover the pan with a lid. Reduce the heat and allow this mixture to continue to cook until the water has evaporated, about 3-4 minutes. Use as required.

SALMON-STYLE FILLET

Believe it or not, fish is one of the easiest flavours to recreate with plant-based ingredients. That's because seaweed provides a remarkably similar taste. This was the starting point for crafting our salmon-style fillets. The next step was to get the texture right. We found the carrot strips, after several hours marinating, take on a texture that's almost indistinguishable from salmon... and it looks remarkably similar. After playing around a little longer with various flavours, we eventually nailed it. So, without further ado, here's another recipe that'll wow everyone you know.

MAKES ENOUGH FOR 4 PIZZAS

2 medium carrots
3 tablespoons extra virgin olive oil
1 tablespoon smoked paprika
1 tablespoon freshly squeezed
   lemon juice
1 tablespoon coconut aminos
1 tablespoon dried seaweed flakes
½ garlic clove, finely chopped
a pinch of chopped dill

Peel the carrots using a vegetable peeler (discard the peelings), then continue to peel long slices of the carrot so you end up with strips.

Mix together the marinade by adding the olive oil, smoked paprika, lemon juice and coconut aminos to a tall container. Mix this together with a handheld blender (or in a food processor). Add the seaweed, garlic and dill and stir this all together.

Place the carrot slices into a wide container, ensuring little-to-no overlap. Pour the marinade evenly over the carrot slices.

Cover the container with clingfilm or a lid, and leave to marinate in the fridge for 12-24 hours before use.

Once ready to use, drain off the marinade and lay the carrot strips on your pizza, or serve on a plate as a side dish. This will keep in the fridge for up to 3 days.

See page 104 for a picture of this topping.

CANNELLINI SAUSAGES

These chunky, thick, Italian-style sausages are packed with amazing flavours. The gentle smokiness from the paprika gives them an almost irresistible flavour, and we routinely have a few of these ready to use in various dishes at home. Try them on pizzas, but feel free to give them a go in anything else you fancy, too, from Italian classics like fried peppers and sausages, to grilling them during your next summer barbecue.

MAKES 4

80ml vegetable stock
170g (drained weight) canned
  cannellini or haricot beans,
  rinsed, then mashed
1 tablespoon nutritional yeast
1 tablespoon coconut aminos
½ tablespoon fennel seeds
1 teaspoon extra virgin olive oil
1 tablespoon finely chopped shallot
1 teaspoon fine pink Himalayan salt
½ garlic clove, finely chopped
½ tablespoon vegan white wine
½ teaspoon smoked paprika
¼ teaspoon freshly ground black pepper
120g rice flour

Mix all the ingredients, except the rice flour, together in a large mixing bowl. At this stage, you can actually customise your sausages beyond the recipe here. If you wish to add particular herbs and spices, you may do so at this point.

Once the flavours are to your liking, add the rice flour and begin mixing with a fork until the mixture is consistent and combined. Knead the mixture together for a further 2-3 minutes - it should lose some stickiness as you do this. If it is still sticky, add a little extra flour. If it becomes too dry, you can counteract this by adding a little extra vegetable stock.

Divide the mixture into four equal portions and place each portion on to a separate piece of foil (large enough to enclose each sausage). Roll each portion into a sausage shape using the foil, rolling the foil around each sausage, then twist the ends of the foil to enclose the sausages completely.

Once wrapped up, you can steam these sausages. Cook them in a steamer for 45 minutes, adding extra water halfway through. If you don't have a steamer, you can cook them in a pan of simmering water for 15 minutes, then drain.

Once cooked, leave the sausages to cool a little, then place them in the fridge for 30-45 minutes to set.

These sausages can then be unwrapped and fried, grilled or cooked on your barbecue, and used in any suitable recipe, from a vegan full English breakfast to a hot dog, but, of course, we have pizza recipes using them in this book, too.

See page 95 for a picture of this topping.

SMOKED CARROT PANCETTA

Pancetta, for many, is the gold standard when it comes to Italian cured meats. It was therefore essential for us to tackle this recipe head on, and create a modern, plant-based version. By combining smoky, salty ingredients like coconut aminos and smoked paprika, you get a flavour that's so similar to pancetta and bacon that it'll have even die-hard carnivores drooling. By applying it to gently roasted carrots, you'll have the texture nailed, too. Ta-da! Plant-based pancetta, ready for your pizzas.

MAKES ENOUGH FOR 4 PIZZAS

1 large carrot, peeled
1½ tablespoons coconut aminos
1 tablespoon smoked paprika
½ tablespoon extra virgin olive oil
50ml sunflower oil
a pinch of fine pink Himalayan salt, to taste

Trim the sides of the carrot to make an oblong shape, then cut the carrot into small cubes about 1cm in size.

In a blender or food processor, blend together the coconut aminos, smoked paprika and olive oil along with 200ml water. Pour this mixture into a large frying pan over a medium-high heat.

Add the carrot cubes, stir to mix, then part cover the pan with the lid and cook, stirring occasionally, for about 10-12 minutes until the water has fully evaporated - watch the pan closely.

Now add the sunflower oil and increase the heat to high. Fry the carrot cubes for a further 2-3 minutes, until the outsides are crispy. Add salt to taste (traditional pancetta has a very salty flavour). Let the cubes cool for 10 minutes before scattering over a pizza or adding to a salad. This will keep in the fridge for up to 3 days.

CARROT PARMA HAM

Traditional Parma ham takes 1-3 years to make, with ham being salted, cured and hung for months and months. Meanwhile, this recipe takes only 20 minutes. By gently frying carrot strips in this rich marinade, we end up with soft and tender plant-based Parma ham, richly flavoured and perfect for salads and pizzas alike. Carrot has an amazing ability to soak up a variety of flavours, and as it cooks here it takes on a texture that's identical to traditional Parma ham. Easy, fast and delicious.

MAKES ENOUGH FOR 4 PIZZAS

1 extra-large carrot
2 tablespoons coconut aminos
½ tablespoon extra virgin olive oil
½ teaspoon fine pink Himalayan salt

Peel the carrot using a vegetable peeler (discard the peelings), then continue to peel long slices of the carrot so you end up with strips.

Add 200ml of water to a large frying pan, along with the coconut aminos, olive oil and salt, and stir to mix.

Submerge the carrot strips in the liquid, trying to avoid overlapping. Now partly cover the pan and cook over a medium-high heat for about 8-10 minutes until the water has completely evaporated, leaving behind a brown residue at the bottom of the pan.

Transfer the carrot strips to a plate and let them cool for 10 minutes before using as required. This will keep in the fridge for up to 3 days.

See page 119 for a picture of this topping.

TUNA-STYLE PLUM TOMATOES

Using one of Italy's finest tomatoes, the Roma tomato, and combining it with a marinade made using seaweed, maple syrup and coconut aminos, we can create a plant-based tuna that tastes irresistible. This one makes appearances again and again for us in all kinds of dishes, from pizzas to cold pasta salads. There's a little bit of Plant Pioneer science needed to get this right – by boiling the tomatoes and then applying ice-cold water, the skin practically melts off. Then it's just a case of marinating them for a short while. Alternatively, use large tomatoes or beef tomatoes.

MAKES ENOUGH FOR 4 PIZZAS

ice cubes (for chilling the water)
4 Roma plum tomatoes
1½ tablespoons coconut aminos
1½ teaspoons rice vinegar
1 tablespoon seaweed (or 1 tablespoon crushed dried nori sheet)
1½ teaspoons maple syrup
½ teaspoon garlic powder (or ½ garlic clove, finely sliced)
¼ teaspoon ground ginger

Fill a medium saucepan with water and bring it to the boil. Pour some cold water into a bowl and add some ice.

Simmer the whole tomatoes in the pan of boiling water for at least 2–3 minutes until you see the skins start to split. Drain the tomatoes, then immediately place them in the bowl of iced water for 20–30 seconds. This will chill them, and the thermal shock will also make the skins easy to peel.

Drain the tomatoes and peel off the skins, then cut them into 3–4cm-thick slices. Remove the seeds with a teaspoon.

Place all the remaining ingredients in a suitable container and mix together. Add the tomato slices, close the lid and gently shake the container to ensure the tomato slices are well coated. Chill in the fridge for at least 2 hours, before serving.

Once ready to use, drain off the marinade and lay the tomatoes on your pizza, or serve them on a plate as a side dish. They will keep in an airtight container in the fridge for up to 3 days.

See page 118 for a picture of this topping.

CHAPTER
5

DRESSINGS & DIPS

With hearty dough comes hearty crusts. Honestly, we could enjoy just a platter of good sourdough crusts... they're one of our favourite parts of any pizza. But they're made all the more enjoyable with a variety of dips to dunk them into, so prep a couple of these to partner up with a pizza.

CHILLI OIL

Any traditional pizzerias will carry chilli oil as an optional addition for your pizzas. A simple drizzle of this warm, aromatic, chilli-infused olive oil provides a little extra heat and a little extra flavour to any pizza, and honestly, we think you'll have a hard time not adding it to pretty much every dish that you love. It's so simple to make, but stick to small batches as it doesn't keep for long. You won't have trouble using it up... trust us!

MAKES 200ML

95ml extra virgin olive oil
95ml sunflower oil
1–2 fresh red chilli(es)
½ garlic clove, peeled
1½ tablespoons dried chilli flakes
¼ teaspoon fine pink Himalayan salt
1½ teaspoons apple cider vinegar

Place all the ingredients, except the vinegar, into a saucepan and begin heating over a medium heat. After about 4 minutes (or when the combined oil reaches its smoke point), remove the pan from the heat and allow the mixture to cool.

Once cool, stir in the vinegar. Pour the chilli oil through a metal sieve into a sterilised glass bottle (or use a slotted spoon to remove the flavourings before pouring the oil into the bottle), then seal and store in a cool, dry place for up to 1 month. Use as required.

Pictured on page 76, number 1.

SMOKED CARAMELISED BEETROOT DIP

A truly gorgeous combination of flavours here. The beetroot provides a moreish sweetness, which merges with the tangy savoury flavours of the red onion and balsamic vinegar. Beetroots are home to a myriad of amazing health benefits, with Olympians even crediting them for legal performance-boosting effects. We're not saying that this dip will turn you into the next Usain Bolt, but this one's pretty much impossible to stop eating.

MAKES 200ML

100g raw beetroot
2 tablespoons extra virgin olive oil
½ tablespoon brown sugar
1 teaspoon balsamic vinegar
1 tablespoon finely chopped red onion
3 tablespoons any plant-based milk
   (but avoid coconut milk)
2 teaspoons smoked paprika
a pinch of fine pink Himalayan salt
3 tablespoons sunflower oil

Peel the beetroot and cut it into small chunks or slices. Heat the olive oil in a small pan over a medium heat, then add the beetroot and cook for 5 minutes until softened.

Remove from the heat, tip the beetroot into a heatproof bowl and stir in the sugar and vinegar. Leave to cool.

Once cool, pour the mixture into a blender or food processor (or use a handheld blender and a bowl) and add the red onion, plant milk, smoked paprika and salt. Turn on the blender, then slowly add the sunflower oil and continue blending until the mixture is smooth and combined.

Use immediately or store in an airtight container in the fridge for up to 3 days.

Pictured on page 76, number 2.

GARLIC MAYONNAISE

This dip is so good that it may turn your pizza crusts into your favourite part of the entire meal. We've seen people at Purezza order several pots of this mayo for a single pizza, generously smothering their crusts in the stuff. It's thick, it's creamy, it's luxurious, and it's a sure-fire hit, whether you're plant-based or not. It's stupendously easy to make, too, meaning we wouldn't blame you if you started covering all of your food in this one.

MAKES 300G

3 tablespoons aquafaba (this is the water from a can of chickpeas)
1 tablespoon freshly squeezed lemon juice
2 teaspoons brown rice syrup
1 teaspoon apple cider vinegar
½ teaspoon fine pink Himalayan salt, to taste
½ garlic clove, finely chopped
¼ teaspoon dry mustard powder
280ml sunflower oil

Add the aquafaba, lemon juice, brown rice syrup, vinegar, salt, garlic and dry mustard powder to a blender or food processor (or use a handheld blender and a bowl). Blend on a low-medium speed, gradually adding the sunflower oil as you blend.

Continue this process until all of the oil is added, and the mixture becomes smooth, white and creamy. If your mayo seems to be too thick, you can add a splash of water and keep mixing.

Transfer the mayo to an airtight container and use as required. This will keep in the fridge for up to 1 week.

Pictured on page 77, number 3.

WILD MUSHROOM DIP

Mushrooms seem to have that whole love-them-or-hate-them thing going on, but for those who adore mushrooms, then it doesn't get much better than this dip. With their deep, rich and earthy tones it's not a surprise that they are so frequently used in Italian cooking - their intense flavour is a gourmet sensation.

MAKES 200G

1 teaspoon extra virgin olive oil
80g wild mushrooms (or porcini), chopped
½ garlic clove, finely chopped
1 teaspoon chopped parsley
a pinch of fine pink Himalayan salt, plus 1 teaspoon
a pinch of freshly ground black pepper
3 tablespoons any plant-based milk (but avoid coconut milk)
a pinch of nutritional yeast
4 tablespoons sunflower oil

Heat the olive oil in a pan. Add the mushrooms and the garlic and fry over a high heat, stirring occasionally, until the mushrooms are beginning to brown and all the juices have evaporated, about 3 minutes. Take the pan off the heat, stir in the parsley, the pinch of salt and the black pepper, then allow the mixture to cool.

Once cool, transfer the mushroom mixture to a blender or food processor (or use a handheld blender and a bowl), along with the milk and blend together until smooth. Add the remaining 1 teaspoon of salt and the nutritional yeast to the blended mixture and blend again.

With the blender running on a slow speed, gradually add the sunflower oil - once this is done, the mixture will be thicker and is then ready to serve.

Use immediately or store in an airtight container in the fridge for up to 3 days.

Pictured on page 77, number 4.

PESTO

The gold standard in pesto. This is the recipe we've honed and tweaked over several years at Purezza, and one that die-hard pesto fanatics have told us is the best pesto they've ever had. Plenty of fresh ingredients make up the core components of this one, but we swap the obviously non-vegan Parmesan with a plant-based alternative: nutritional yeast. These cheesy, nutty-flavoured flakes make for a wonderful (and healthy) addition to this classic Italian recipe.

MAKES 200G

100g basil
2 tablespoons pine nuts
½ garlic clove, peeled
3½ tablespoons extra virgin olive oil
2 tablespoons nutritional yeast
1 teaspoon fine pink Himalayan salt

Add all the ingredients to a blender or food processor. Blend together until you get a creamy, liquid consistency. Serve!

Store any leftovers in an airtight container in the fridge for up to 3 days.

Pictured on page 76, number 5.

TAPENADE

Few dishes have stood the test of time quite like tapenade. The first known instance of a tapenade recipe being recorded was in Cato the Elder's De Agri Cultura, the oldest surviving Latin prose dating back to approximately 160 BC. It has, of course, evolved over time, but for us this is the ultimate tapenade recipe, using the very best Italian olives you can buy.

It's very flexible as a dip – it works with crackers, breadsticks, cooked pizza dough, bread, etc. – but can also be spread on food such as mild vegetables. A bowl of this stuff and a bottle of wine is a perfect way to while away a summer's evening.

MAKES 200G

80g pitted black olives
80g pitted green olives
1 tablespoon capers, drained
2 garlic cloves, peeled
2 tablespoons extra virgin olive oil
1 teaspoon freshly squeezed lemon juice
¼ teaspoon freshly ground black pepper

Add all the ingredients to a blender or food processor. Pulse-blend on a slow setting, for a few seconds at a time, until you achieve the right consistency, tasting and stirring as you go. Tapenade should not be served smooth, it should be chunky and have some texture.

Serve the tapenade in a bowl to be used as a dip, or to be spread on toasted bread or a baguette. Any leftovers will keep in an airtight container in the fridge for up to 3 days.

Pictured on page 77, number 6.

CHAPTER 6

PIZZAS

Pizza is what we are most well known for at Purezza. The breadth of our
creativity along with our deep obsession with perfection is how we got there.
With awards at both national and international levels, we're proud to be
reinventing this dish we love for a new era. Here is a selection of our favourite
pizza recipes. We innovate on a few classics, we have a few from our restaurants,
and a few that are exclusive to this book. We know you'll love them all.
So the question for you is: which one will you make first?

MARINARA PIZZA

The original Neapolitan pizza, and some in Italy would still attest to it being the very best. In fact, many of the most stalwart pizzerias in Naples continue to cook just the Marinara and the Margherita.

Despite being a recipe that's nearly 300 years old, the Marinara continues to be enjoyed the world over today. To quote one of Italy's greatest minds, Leonardo Da Vinci, 'simplicity is the ultimate sophistication'. You can see why with this classic recipe.

MAKES 1 PIZZA

semolina flour or rice flour, for dusting
1 dough ball (see pages 12–21)
120ml San Marzano Plum Tomato and
   Basil 'Passata' Sauce (see page 24)
1 garlic clove, finely sliced
a pinch of dried oregano
extra virgin olive oil, for drizzling
3–4 basil leaves

Turn the oven to the highest temperature setting, place a pizza stone on the highest shelf in the oven and leave it to heat for at least 1 hour (once the oven has reached full temperature) before baking your pizza.

Generously dust the work surface with flour and flour your hands. Place the dough ball on the work surface and coat it with flour, then shape it by flattening and stretching it using your fingers to make your base (you are aiming for a flat base with slightly thicker, raised edges to make the crust). Pick the pizza base up and gently stretch it a little further over your fists without tearing it. Brush off any excess flour.

Sprinkle a little flour on a pizza peel and gently place the pizza base onto it. Pour the tomato sauce onto the centre of the base and spread it evenly using the bottom of a ladle or tablespoon.

Sprinkle the garlic slices evenly over the sauce. Add the dried oregano and a drizzle of olive oil.

Transfer the pizza to the hot stone in the oven and cook for 6–7 minutes at 240°C (gas mark 9), or for 5–6 minutes if the oven can reach 250°C (gas mark 10).

Once the pizza is ready, remove it from the oven using the pizza peel. Lay the basil leaves on top and add an extra tiny drizzle of olive oil. Serve and enjoy!

Pictured on page 85, number 1.

MARGHERITA PIZZA

Pizza Margherita is one of the most traditional Neapolitan pizzas, first invented to honour the Queen of Italy, Margherita of Savoy, as well as to celebrate the Italian unification. A simple dish with only three toppings, which were created to represent the Italian flag: tomato (red), mozzarella (white) and basil (green).

Every beginner starts by making a Margherita pizza before taking on other toppings, which require more preparation time. This plant-based version of Margherita pizza adds a nutty and creamy taste to the benchmark of Neapolitan tradition.

MAKES 1 PIZZA

semolina flour or rice flour, for dusting
1 dough ball (see pages 12-21)
80ml San Marzano Plum Tomato and
   Basil 'Passata' Sauce (see page 24)
3-4 basil leaves
50-60g Cashew Mozzarella (see page
   40) or Cashew Buffalo Mozzarella
   (see page 46)
extra virgin olive oil, for drizzling

Turn the oven to the highest temperature setting, place a pizza stone on the highest shelf in the oven and leave it to heat for at least 1 hour (once the oven has reached full temperature) before baking your pizza.

Generously dust the work surface with flour and flour your hands. Place the dough ball on the work surface and coat it with flour, then shape it by flattening and stretching it using your fingers to make your base (you are aiming for a flat base with slightly thicker, raised edges to make the crust). Pick the pizza base up and gently stretch it a little further over your fists without tearing it. Brush off any excess flour.

Sprinkle a little flour on a pizza peel and gently place the pizza base onto it. Pour the tomato sauce onto the centre of the base and spread it evenly using the bottom of a ladle or tablespoon.

Transfer the pizza to the hot stone in the oven and cook for 6 minutes at 240°C (gas mark 9), or for 5 minutes if the oven can reach 250°C (gas mark 10).

Remove the pizza from the oven using the pizza peel. Scatter the basil leaves over the pizza, spread the mozzarella evenly on top, then return the pizza to the oven to cook for a further 1 minute.

Once the pizza is ready, take it out of the oven, add a drizzle of olive oil and enjoy!

Pictured on page 84, number 2.

SIX CHEESE PIZZA

Of all the pizzas in a vegan cookbook, this is the one that raises the most eyebrows. 'Six cheeses' and 'plant-based' don't seem like they go together very well! However, all it requires is a shift in our understanding to see that we can make beautiful artisanal cheeses using plant-based ingredients alone. This pizza will have jaws dropping when your guests find out there's no dairy in it whatsoever.

MAKES 1 PIZZA

semolina flour or rice flour, for dusting
1 dough ball (see pages 12-21)
50g Spreadable Cheese (see page 45)
25ml any plant-based milk (but avoid coconut milk) or water
extra virgin olive oil, for drizzling
a few basil leaves, plus 3-4 extra to garnish
50g Almond Gorgonzola Cheese (see page 41)
50g Cashew and Walnut Pecorino, grated (see page 44)
50g Cashew Mozzarella (see page 40) or Cashew Buffalo Mozzarella (see page 46)
50g Almond Ricotta (see page 45)

TO FINISH
a pinch of nutritional yeast
a pinch of Grated Nut Parmesan (see page 41)
a drizzle of extra virgin olive oil

Turn the oven to the highest temperature setting, place a pizza stone on the highest shelf in the oven and leave it to heat for at least 1 hour (once the oven has reached full temperature) before baking your pizza.

Generously dust the work surface with flour and flour your hands. Place the dough ball on the work surface and coat it with flour, then shape it by flattening and stretching it using your fingers to make your base (you are aiming for a flat base with slightly thicker, raised edges to make the crust). Pick the pizza base up and gently stretch it a little further over your fists without tearing it. Brush off any excess flour.

Sprinkle a little flour on the pizza peel and gently place the pizza base onto it. Mix the spreadable cheese with the plant-based milk or water and gently spread the mixture over the base (starting from the centre) using the bottom of a ladle. Add a drizzle of olive oil.

Transfer the pizza to the hot stone in the oven and cook for 6 minutes at 240°C (gas mark 9), or for 5 minutes if the oven can reach 250°C (gas mark 10).

Remove the pizza from the oven using the pizza peel. Scatter a few basil leaves over the pizza, place all the cheeses evenly on top (dolloping the ricotta on as you go), then return the pizza to the oven to cook for a further 1 minute.

Once the pizza is ready, take it out of the oven. Sprinkle over the nutritional yeast, Parmesan and 3-4 basil leaves to garnish, add a final drizzle of olive oil and enjoy!

Pictured on page 84, number 3.

FOUR SEASONS PIZZA

The *quattro stagioni*, or four seasons pizza, is perhaps one of the most famous in all of Italian cuisine, and thus it's one that we had to apply our Plant Pioneer talents to. The four core ingredients represent winter, spring, summer and autumn, but it's a winner all year round for us.

MAKES 1 PIZZA

semolina flour or rice flour, for dusting
1 dough ball (see pages 12–21)
80ml San Marzano Plum Tomato and
    Basil 'Passata' Sauce (see page 24)
35g Smoked Beetroot Carpaccio
    (see page 57)
40g artichoke heart quarters from a jar,
    drained
25g pitted black olives, left whole
40g Funghi Trifolati (see page 54)
50g Cashew Mozzarella (see page 40)
    or Cashew Buffalo Mozzarella
    (see page 46)

TO FINISH
3–4 basil leaves
a drizzle of extra virgin olive oil

Turn the oven to the highest temperature setting, place a pizza stone on the highest shelf in the oven and leave it to heat for at least 1 hour (once the oven has reached full temperature) before baking your pizza.

Generously dust the work surface with flour and flour your hands. Place the dough ball on the work surface and coat it with flour, then shape it by flattening and stretching it using your fingers to make your base (you are aiming for a flat base with slightly thicker, raised edges to make the crust). Pick the pizza base up and gently stretch it a little further over your fists without tearing it. Brush off any excess flour.

Sprinkle a little flour on the pizza peel and gently place the pizza base onto it. Pour the tomato sauce onto the centre of the base and spread it evenly using the bottom of a ladle or tablespoon. Add the remaining ingredients evenly to the base, except the mozzarella, basil and olive oil, placing each ingredient over one separate quarter of the base (so you end up with four different, separate topping quarters over the base).

Transfer the pizza to the hot stone in the oven and cook for 6 minutes at 240°C (gas mark 9), or for 5 minutes if the oven can reach 250°C (gas mark 10).

Remove the pizza from the oven using the pizza peel. Spread the mozzarella evenly on top of the pizza, then return it to the oven to cook for a further 1 minute.

Once the pizza is ready, take it out of the oven, scatter over the basil leaves and a drizzle of olive oil to finish, and enjoy!

Pictured on page 85, number 4.

BUTTERNUT SQUASH AND CAVOLO NERO PIZZA

- WITH CARAMELISED ONIONS -

Cavolo nero literally translates as 'black cabbage'. It's a variety of kale traditionally used in Italian cuisine, especially in Tuscany, where for centuries it has been one of the main ingredients for making minestrone and *ribollita*. Its slightly bitter taste marries well with the sweetness of the butternut squash and caramelised onions, making this pizza a winter winner! Cavolo nero is available in many supermarkets and it often comes pre-chopped. Alternatively, use kale.

MAKES 1 PIZZA

semolina flour or rice flour, for dusting
1 dough ball (see pages 12–21)
80ml Butternut Squash Sauce
 (see page 28)
50g Caramelised Onions (see page 51)

FOR THE CAVOLO NERO
75g cavolo nero, washed
1 tablespoon extra virgin olive oil
½ garlic clove, peeled
1 tablespoon vegan white wine
a pinch of salt
a pinch of freshly ground black pepper

TO FINISH
½ tablespoon sunflower oil
20g pumpkin seeds
½ teaspoon coconut aminos
a pinch of fine pink Himalayan salt

Turn the oven to the highest temperature setting, place a pizza stone on the highest shelf in the oven and leave it to heat for at least 1 hour (once the oven has reached full temperature) before baking your pizza.

Prepare the cavolo nero. Remove the stalks and thickly slice the leaves. Heat the olive oil in a pan over a medium heat for 30 seconds. Add the garlic and cook for 30 seconds, stirring, then discard the garlic. Add the cavolo nero and wine and cook for 1 minute, then add the salt and pepper and stir for a few seconds. Remove from the heat and set aside.

Generously dust the work surface with flour and flour your hands. Place the dough ball on the work surface and coat it with flour, then shape it by flattening and stretching it using your fingers to make your base (you are aiming for a flat base with slightly thicker, raised edges to make the crust). Pick the pizza base up and gently stretch it a little further over your fists without tearing it. Brush off any excess flour.

Sprinkle a little flour on a pizza peel and gently place the pizza base onto it. Pour the butternut squash sauce onto the centre of the base and spread it evenly using the bottom of a ladle or tablespoon, then top evenly with the caramelised onions and cavolo nero.

Transfer the pizza to the hot stone in the oven and cook for 6–7 minutes at 240°C (gas mark 9), or for 5–6 minutes if the oven can reach 250°C (gas mark 10).

Meanwhile, prepare the garnish. Heat the sunflower oil in a small pan over a medium heat for 1 minute, add the pumpkin seeds and stir until they become toasted, 1–2 minutes. Add the coconut aminos and stir briefly until it has reduced. Add the salt and stir for a few seconds. Turn off the heat.

Once the pizza is ready, remove it from the oven using the pizza peel. Garnish with the seed mixture, then serve and enjoy!

MONTANARA PIZZA

- FRIED PIZZA WITH MARINARA SAUCE, BASIL AND PARMESAN -

The idea of a deep-fried pizza should get everyone's stomach rumbling, but the Montanara actually forms a truly traditional part of Neapolitan heritage. As its name suggests, it hails from the mountains surrounding Naples itself, where it was commonplace to dunk pizza dough into hot oil before topping it. The result is just as luxurious as you can probably imagine – soft, chewy dough surrounded by a light and crispy coating. You are welcome to play around with fried dough, but here's a recipe for the traditional Montanara, given a few Plant Pioneer tweaks along the way, of course.

MAKES 1 PIZZA

sunflower oil, for deep-frying
semolina flour or rice flour, for dusting
½ dough ball (see pages 12–21)
1½ tablespoons Marinara Sauce
    (see page 26)

TO FINISH
1 teaspoon Grated Nut Parmesan
    (see page 41)
nutritional yeast, for sprinkling
a few basil leaves

Put enough sunflower oil in a deep pan to three-quarters fill it (or use a deep-fat fryer) and heat the oil to a temperature of 180°C or until a cube of bread browns in 30 seconds.

Generously dust the work surface with flour and flour your hands. Place the half dough ball on the work surface and coat it with flour, then shape it by flattening and stretching it using your fingers to make your base (you are aiming for an even thickness of 2–3mm – you need to ensure it's not too thin, especially in the middle). Pick the pizza base up and brush off any excess flour.

Carefully place the pizza base into the hot oil, frying it for about 30 seconds on each side until cooked and golden. Remove the pizza base and place it on a kitchen paper-lined plate to remove the excess oil from both sides.

Transfer the pizza base to a serving plate, then pour the marinara sauce onto the centre of the pizza, using the bottom of a spoon to spread it evenly (if you like, you can gently heat the marinara sauce beforehand, but it is not essential). Sprinkle the grated nut Parmesan and nutritional yeast over the top, and then scatter the basil leaves over before eating.

ASPARAGUS, BABY PLUM TOMATO AND PISTACHIO PIZZA

The two core ingredients of asparagus and pistachios leave this pizza feeling relatively light, yet both are rich in flavour, too, and they're packed with great nutritional qualities. From around late April until mid-June, asparagus is in season in the UK, so aim to get hold of some from a local farmers' market, and give this refreshing pizza a go.

MAKES 1 PIZZA

semolina flour or rice flour, for dusting
1 dough ball (see pages 12-21)
50g baby plum tomatoes, quartered
50-60g Cashew Mozzarella (see page 40) or Cashew Buffalo Mozzarella (see page 46)
crushed pistachio nuts, to garnish

FOR THE ASPARAGUS

1 tablespoon extra virgin olive oil, plus extra for drizzling
1 garlic clove, finely chopped
75g seasonal asparagus, woody ends trimmed off, spears cut into 2-3cm lengths
1 tablespoon vegan white wine
a pinch of fine pink Himalayan salt
a pinch of freshly ground black pepper, plus an extra pinch to serve

Turn the oven to the highest temperature setting, place a pizza stone on the highest shelf in the oven and leave it to heat for at least 1 hour (once the oven has reached full temperature) before baking your pizza.

Prepare the asparagus. Heat the olive oil in a pan over a medium heat for 30 seconds, then add the garlic and asparagus and cook for 1 minute, stirring. Next, add the wine and cook for 1 minute. Finally, add the salt and black pepper and stir for a few seconds. Take the pan off the heat whilst the asparagus is still crunchy.

Generously dust the work surface with flour and flour your hands. Place the dough ball on the work surface and coat it with flour, then shape it by flattening and stretching it using your fingers to make your base (you are aiming for a flat base with slightly thicker, raised edges to make the crust). Pick the pizza base up and gently stretch it a little further over your fists without tearing it. Brush off any excess flour.

Sprinkle a little flour on the pizza peel and gently place the pizza base onto it. Add the asparagus and tomatoes evenly to the base and drizzle over a little olive oil.

Transfer the pizza to the hot stone in the oven and cook for 6 minutes at 240°C (gas mark 9), or for 5 minutes if the oven can reach 250°C (gas mark 10).

Remove the pizza from the oven using the pizza peel. Spread the mozzarella evenly on top of the pizza, then return it to the oven to cook for a further 1 minute.

Once the pizza is ready, take it out of the oven, then add the crushed pistachios, a pinch of black pepper and a drizzle of olive oil. Enjoy!

Pictured on page 94, number 1.

TENDERSTEM BROCCOLI AND SAUSAGE PIZZA

This one is loosely based on an Italian classic, *Salsiccia e Friarielli*, which uses sausage and Italian broccoli. We use freshly grown tenderstem broccoli - a variety that works remarkably well in pizza, offering a satisfying texture and gentle crunch. By then applying a bit of Plant Pioneer magic to the sausages, we have a piece of Neapolitan tradition that's truly modernised with vegan and locally sourced ingredients.

MAKES 1 PIZZA

semolina flour or rice flour, for dusting
1 dough ball (see pages 12–21)
75g Stir-fried Wild Broccoli (see page 61)
40g cooked Cannellini Sausages
　(see page 64), crumbled
extra virgin olive oil, for drizzling
50–60g Cashew Mozzarella (see page
　40) or Cashew Buffalo Mozzarella
　(see page 46)
a pinch of dried chilli flakes, to garnish

Turn the oven to the highest temperature setting, place a pizza stone on the highest shelf in the oven and leave it to heat for at least 1 hour (once the oven has reached full temperature) before baking your pizza.

Generously dust the work surface with flour and flour your hands. Place the dough ball on the work surface and coat it with flour, then shape it by flattening and stretching it using your fingers to make your base (you are aiming for a flat base with slightly thicker, raised edges to make the crust). Pick the pizza base up and gently stretch it a little further over your fists without tearing it. Brush off any excess flour.

Sprinkle a little flour on the pizza peel and gently place the pizza base onto it. Add the broccoli and sausages evenly to the base, then drizzle over some olive oil.

Transfer the pizza to the hot stone in the oven and cook for 6 minutes at 240°C (gas mark 9), or for 5 minutes if the oven can reach 250°C (gas mark 10).

Remove the pizza from the oven using the pizza peel. Spread the mozzarella evenly on top of the pizza, then return it to the oven to cook for a further 1 minute.

Once the pizza is ready, take it out of the oven, scatter over the chilli flakes to garnish, add another drizzle of olive oil and enjoy!

Pictured on page 95, number 2.

PARMIGIANA PIZZA

A modern day classic. This is the pizza that won Purezza the National Pizza of the Year award in 2018, and here's the recipe in full for you to recreate it at home. This takes a classic aubergine parmigiana, and weaves it into a pizza dish. The result is gloriously sloppy and undeniably delicious. Routinely deemed to be the best pizza on our whole menu by our customers, this is heaven on a plate.

MAKES 1 PIZZA

semolina flour or rice flour, for dusting
1 dough ball (see pages 12-21)
80ml San Marzano Plum Tomato and Basil 'Passata' Sauce (see page 24)
125g Parmigiana (see page 53)
30g cooked Cannellini Sausages (see page 64), crumbled
50g Cashew Mozzarella (see page 40) or Cashew Buffalo Mozzarella (see page 46)

TO FINISH
3-4 basil leaves
a drizzle of extra virgin olive oil
a pinch of nutritional yeast

Turn the oven to the highest temperature setting, place a pizza stone on the highest shelf in the oven and leave it to heat for at least 1 hour (once the oven has reached full temperature) before baking your pizza.

Generously dust the work surface with flour and flour your hands. Place the dough ball on the work surface and coat it with flour, then shape it by flattening and stretching it using your fingers to make your base (you are aiming for a flat base with slightly thicker, raised edges to make the crust). Pick the pizza base up and gently stretch it a little further over your fists without tearing it. Brush off any excess flour.

Sprinkle a little flour on the pizza peel and gently place the pizza base onto it. Pour the tomato sauce onto the centre of the base and spread it evenly using the bottom of a ladle or tablespoon.

Transfer the pizza to the hot stone in the oven and cook for 6 minutes at 240°C (gas mark 9), or for 5 minutes if the oven can reach 250°C (gas mark 10).

Remove the pizza from the oven using the pizza peel. Place the parmigiana and crumbled sausages evenly on top of the pizza, then add the mozzarella, ensuring some of it covers the sausages, too. Return the pizza to the oven to cook for a further 1 minute.

Once the pizza is ready, take it out of the oven, scatter over the basil leaves, drizzle over a little olive oil and sprinkle over the nutritional yeast to finish - congrats... you've just made the National Pizza of the Year 2018. Tuck in!

Pictured on page 95, number 3.

AUBERGINE 'MEATBALLS' PIZZA

Aubergines might just be one of the most versatile foods in the whole world, and this pizza certainly furthers that claim. The meatball pizza was actually invented by New York's Italian community, but is now a regular on the menu at many of Italy's best pizzerias. Our amazing meatballs are easy to make and delicious. Make a few extra and enjoy them with some spaghetti for another Italian treat.

MAKES 1 PIZZA

semolina flour or rice flour, for dusting
1 dough ball (see pages 12-21)
80ml Marinara Sauce (see page 26)
40g Melanzane 'a Funghetto'
   (see page 50)
5-8 Aubergine 'Meatballs' (see page 52),
   cooked
50g Cashew Mozzarella (see page 40)
   or Cashew Buffalo Mozzarella
   (see page 46)

TO FINISH
a few basil leaves
a drizzle of extra virgin olive oil
a pinch of nutritional yeast

Turn the oven to the highest temperature setting, place a pizza stone on the highest shelf in the oven and leave it to heat for at least 1 hour (once the oven has reached full temperature) before baking your pizza.

Generously dust the work surface with flour and flour your hands. Place the dough ball on the work surface and coat it with flour, then shape it by flattening and stretching it using your fingers to make your base (you are aiming for a flat base with slightly thicker, raised edges to make the crust). Pick the pizza base up and gently stretch it a little further over your fists without tearing it. Brush off any excess flour.

Sprinkle a little flour on the pizza peel and gently place the pizza base onto it. Pour the marinara sauce onto the centre of the base and spread it evenly using the bottom of a ladle or tablespoon, then evenly spoon the melanzane over the sauce.

Transfer the pizza to the hot stone in the oven and cook for 6 minutes at 240°C (gas mark 9), or for 5 minutes if the oven can reach 250°C (gas mark 10).

Remove the pizza from the oven using the pizza peel. Place the meatballs over the base, then top with the mozzarella, placing some mozzarella on top of the meatballs, too. Return the pizza to the oven to cook for a further 1 minute.

Once the pizza is ready, take it out of the oven, scatter over the basil leaves, a drizzle of olive oil and the nutritional yeast to finish, then serve.

Pictured on page 94, number 4.

MIXED MUSHROOM AND SAUSAGE PIZZA

- WITH BLACK TRUFFLE -

Truffles are tubers often associated with mushrooms, as they both belong to the fungi family. However, when it comes to the taste, they are nothing alike. Many chefs refer to them as the 'diamond of the kitchen' and often exalt their aromatic, earthy, pungent and deliciously funky taste. In Italy, they are mainly found in the Umbria, Marche and Tuscany regions and are used in a variety of recipes, including pasta dishes and pizzas. Combined with *funghi trifolati* (sautéd mushrooms) and cashew mozzarella, they make an exceptional pizza!

MAKES 1 PIZZA

semolina flour or rice flour, for dusting
1 dough ball (see pages 12–21)
75g Funghi Trifolati (see page 54)
35g cooked Cannellini Sausages
    (see page 64), crumbled
50-60g Cashew Mozzarella
    (see page 40) or Cashew Buffalo
    Mozzarella (see page 46)

TO FINISH
a few rocket leaves
a few thin slices of black truffle
a drizzle of extra virgin olive oil

Turn the oven to the highest temperature setting, place a pizza stone on the highest shelf in the oven and leave it to heat for at least 1 hour (once the oven has reached full temperature) before baking your pizza.

Generously dust the work surface with flour and flour your hands. Place the dough ball on the work surface and coat it with flour, then shape it by flattening and stretching it using your fingers to make your base (you are aiming for a flat base with slightly thicker, raised edges to make the crust). Pick the pizza base up and gently stretch it a little further over your fists without tearing it. Brush off any excess flour.

Sprinkle a little flour on the pizza peel and gently place the pizza base on to it. Add the mushrooms and crumbled sausages evenly to the base.

Transfer the pizza to the hot stone in the oven and cook for 6 minutes at 240°C (gas mark 9), or for 5 minutes if the oven can reach 250°C (gas mark 10).

Remove the pizza from the oven using the pizza peel. Spread the mozzarella evenly on top of the pizza, then return it to the oven to cook for a further 1 minute.

Once the pizza is ready, take it out of the oven, scatter over the rocket leaves and truffle slices, add a drizzle of olive oil and enjoy!

ROASTED POTATO AND SMOKED CARROT PANCETTA PIZZA

Whilst potato on pizza seems like an odd partnership, the core elements of this recipe date back decades and decades. *Pizza con patate* has been a much-loved Neapolitan delicacy for several generations. It uses a white base (meaning no tomato sauce), and is sprinkled with flavour-rich herbs. We add some plant-based pancetta, and the result is a comfort food classic.

MAKES 1 PIZZA

semolina flour or rice flour, for dusting
1 dough ball (see pages 12–21)
extra virgin olive oil, for drizzling
50g Roasted Potatoes with Garlic and
  Rosemary (see page 57)
50g Smoked Carrot Pancetta
  (see page 65)
50g Cashew Mozzarella (see page 40)
  or Cashew Buffalo Mozzarella
  (see page 46)

TO FINISH
3–4 basil leaves
a pinch of freshly ground black pepper

Turn the oven to the highest temperature setting, place a pizza stone on the highest shelf in the oven and leave it to heat for at least 1 hour (once the oven has reached full temperature) before baking your pizza.

Generously dust the work surface with flour and flour your hands. Place the dough ball on the work surface and coat it with flour, then shape it by flattening and stretching it using your fingers to make your base (you are aiming for a flat base with slightly thicker, raised edges to make the crust). Pick the pizza base up and gently stretch it a little further over your fists without tearing it. Brush off any excess flour.

Sprinkle a little flour on the pizza peel and gently place the pizza base onto it. Drizzle some olive oil over the whole base, spiralling outwards from the centre as you drizzle. Add the potatoes evenly to the base.

Transfer the pizza to the hot stone in the oven and cook for 6 minutes at 240°C (gas mark 9), or for 5 minutes if the oven can reach 250°C (gas mark 10).

Remove the pizza from the oven using the pizza peel. Place the pancetta evenly over the top of the pizza, then add the mozzarella, ensuring some of it covers the pancetta, too. Return the pizza to the oven to cook for a further 1 minute.

Once the pizza is ready, take it out of the oven, scatter over the basil leaves, drizzle over a little olive oil and sprinkle over the black pepper to finish. Serve and enjoy!

FUNGHI TRIFOLATI AND SUN-DRIED TOMATO PESTO PIZZA

- WITH PEA SAUCE -

Fresh, rich springtime flavours unite on this pizza. One of the most aesthetically beautiful pizzas in this whole book, with colours reminiscent of the Italian flag, it packs plenty of flavour to match up to its looks. The mild and refreshing pea sauce forms a base on which the rich and earthy walnuts and *funghi trifolati* combine with the sharper flavour of the sun-dried tomato pesto. All of these flavours dance for the attention of your taste buds, and the end result is truly delicious.

MAKES 1 PIZZA

semolina flour or rice flour, for dusting
1 dough ball (see pages 12–21)
50ml Pea Sauce (see page 30)
50g Funghi Trifolati (see page 54)
50g Cashew Mozzarella (see page 40)
   or Cashew Buffalo Mozzarella
   (see page 46)

TO FINISH
30g Sun-dried Tomato Pesto Sauce
   (see page 27)
a pinch of chopped parsley
a small handful of crushed walnuts

Turn the oven to the highest temperature setting, place a pizza stone on the highest shelf in the oven and leave it to heat for at least 1 hour (once the oven has reached full temperature) before baking your pizza.

Generously dust the work surface with flour and flour your hands. Place the dough ball on the work surface and coat it with flour, then shape it by flattening and stretching it using your fingers to make your base (you are aiming for a flat base with slightly thicker, raised edges to make the crust). Pick the pizza base up and gently stretch it a little further over your fists without tearing it. Brush off any excess flour.

Sprinkle a little flour on the pizza peel and gently place the pizza base onto it. Pour the pea sauce onto the centre of the base and spread it evenly using the bottom of a ladle or tablespoon, then evenly spoon the mushrooms over the sauce.

Transfer the pizza to the hot stone in the oven and cook for 6 minutes at 240°C (gas mark 9), or for 5 minutes if the oven can reach 250°C (gas mark 10).

Remove the pizza from the oven using the pizza peel. Spread the mozzarella evenly on top of the pizza, then return it to the oven to cook for a further 1 minute.

Once the pizza is ready, take it out of the oven. Using a small squeezy bottle, drizzle a generous zigzag of the sun-dried tomato pesto over the top (if the pesto is too thick, mix in a splash of rice milk first to create a smooth cream), then sprinkle over the parsley and crushed walnuts to finish. Serve and enjoy!

SALMON-STYLE FILLET AND YELLOW TOMATO PIZZA

- WITH CHEESE SAUCE -

Inspired by the classic combo of herby cream cheese and salmon, this pizza captures that much-loved flavour combination atop a glorious sourdough pizza base, using modern plant-based alternatives that are healthier and better for the world. Be sure to give yourself time to marinate the carrot-based 'salmon', and prepare the cheese sauce in advance. We love micro herbs for their ability to provide punchy flavours without taking up much pizza real-estate, leaving room for other toppings - that's why micro parsley is a hit on this one.

MAKES 1 PIZZA

semolina flour or rice flour, for dusting
1 dough ball (see pages 12–21)
50g Spreadable Cheese with Capers and Chives (see page 45)
25ml any plant-based milk (but avoid coconut milk) or water
40g yellow cherry or baby plum tomatoes, quartered
extra virgin olive oil, for drizzling
50g Cashew Mozzarella (see page 40) or Cashew Buffalo Mozzarella (see page 46)
50g Salmon-style Fillet (see page 63)

TO FINISH
a pinch of micro parsley
a pinch of freshly ground black pepper

Turn the oven to the highest temperature setting, place a pizza stone on the highest shelf in the oven and leave it to heat for at least 1 hour (once the oven has reached full temperature) before baking your pizza.

Generously dust the work surface with flour and flour your hands. Place the dough ball on the work surface and coat it with flour, then shape it by flattening and stretching it using your fingers to make your base (you are aiming for a flat base with slightly thicker, raised edges to make the crust). Pick the pizza base up and gently stretch it a little further over your fists without tearing it. Brush off any excess flour.

Sprinkle a little flour on the pizza peel and gently place the pizza base onto it. In a small bowl, whisk together the spreadable cheese with the milk or water, then gently pour this mixture onto the centre of the base and spread evenly using the bottom of a ladle or tablespoon. Top the pizza evenly with the yellow cherry tomatoes or baby plum tomatoes and add a drizzle of olive oil.

Transfer the pizza to the hot stone in the oven and cook for 6 minutes at 240°C (gas mark 9), or for 5 minutes if the oven can reach 250°C (gas mark 10).

Remove the pizza from the oven using the pizza peel. Spread the mozzarella evenly over the top of the pizza, then return it to the oven to cook for a further 1 minute.

Once the pizza is ready, take it out of the oven. Arrange the salmon-style fillet on top, and finish with the micro parsley, black pepper and a drizzle of olive oil. Enjoy!

Pictured on page 104, number 1.

SPINACH AND RICOTTA PIZZA

- WITH MUSHROOM DRESSING -

Spinach and ricotta. It's one of those iconic flavour duos that is more than the sum of its parts, and so well paired that it becomes difficult to imagine one without the other. This creamy, smooth, plant-based ricotta pairs just as well with wilted spinach as its dairy-based counterpart. Mushrooms make for a great final addition to this pizza, giving an extra layer of rich, earthy flavour.

MAKES 1 PIZZA

40g Almond Ricotta (see page 45)
3 tablespoons Wild Mushroom Dip (see page 75)
semolina flour or rice flour, for dusting
1 dough ball (see pages 12-21)
50g San Marzano Plum Tomato and Basil 'Passata' Sauce (see page 24)
extra virgin olive oil, for drizzling
50g Cashew Mozzarella (see page 40) or Cashew Buffalo Mozzarella (see page 46)

FOR THE SPINACH

1 teaspoon extra virgin olive oil
½ garlic clove, peeled
100g fresh baby spinach leaves, washed
a pinch of fine pink Himalayan salt

TO FINISH

a pinch of chopped parsley
a pinch of freshly ground black pepper

Turn the oven to the highest temperature setting, place a pizza stone on the highest shelf in the oven and leave it to heat for at least 1 hour (once the oven has reached full temperature) before baking your pizza.

Prepare the spinach. Heat the olive oil in a pan over a medium heat for 30 seconds. Add the garlic and cook for 30 seconds, stirring, then discard. Add the still-wet spinach and cook for 1 minute, stirring occasionally, then add the salt and stir for a few seconds. Remove from the heat and set aside.

Spoon the ricotta into a disposable piping bag and snip off the tip to make a medium-sized hole. Spoon the mushroom dip into a small squeezy bottle.

Generously dust the work surface with flour and flour your hands. Place the dough ball on the work surface and coat it with flour, then shape it by flattening and stretching it using your fingers to make your base (you are aiming for a flat base with slightly thicker, raised edges to make the crust). Pick the pizza base up and gently stretch it a little further over your fists without tearing it. Brush off any excess flour.

Sprinkle a little flour on the pizza peel and gently place the pizza base onto it. Pour the tomato sauce onto the centre of the base and spread it using the bottom of a ladle or tablespoon, then add a drizzle of olive oil.

Transfer the pizza to the hot stone in the oven and cook for 6 minutes at 240°C (gas mark 9), or for 5 minutes if the oven can reach 250°C (gas mark 10).

Remove the pizza from the oven using the pizza peel. Place the spinach evenly over the pizza base, followed by the mozzarella, then pipe six or seven blobs of ricotta on top. Return the pizza to the oven to cook for a further 1 minute.

Once the pizza is ready, take it out of the oven. Drizzle a large zigzag of the mushroom dip over the top, then garnish with the parsley and black pepper. Finish with a drizzle of olive oil and serve.

Pictured on page 105, number 2.

CHICKPEA, LEMON AND MUSHROOM PIZZA

- WITH SMOKED CARROT PANCETTA -

This is one of the zestiest pizzas in the book. Lemon and pancetta dance around on this pizza giving it a unique punchy, yet delicious flavour. All the while, there's a backdrop of rich and earthy mushrooms and chickpeas, both of which complement the lemon and pancetta, providing a full range of flavours for your taste buds to enjoy. We adore this one in summer, when the fresh flavours seem most apt.
Pair it with a side salad and you're good to go.

MAKES 1 PIZZA

semolina flour or rice flour, for dusting
1 dough ball (see pages 12–21)
50g Chickpea and Lemon Sauce
  (see page 34)
50g Funghi Trifolati (see page 54)
extra virgin olive oil, for drizzling
50g Smoked Carrot Pancetta (see page 65)
50g Cashew Mozzarella (see page 40)
  or Cashew Buffalo Mozzarella
  (see page 46)

TO FINISH
1 tablespoon chopped parsley
1 teaspoon finely grated lemon zest
a pinch of freshly ground black pepper

Turn the oven to the highest temperature setting, place a pizza stone on the highest shelf in the oven and leave it to heat for at least 1 hour (once the oven has reached full temperature) before baking your pizza.

Generously dust the work surface with flour and flour your hands. Place the dough ball on the work surface and coat it with flour, then shape it by flattening and stretching it using your fingers to make your base (you are aiming for a flat base with slightly thicker/raised edges to make the crust). Pick the pizza base up and gently stretch it a little further over your fists without tearing it. Brush off any excess flour.

Sprinkle a little flour on the pizza peel and gently place the pizza base on to it. Pour the chickpea sauce on to the centre of the base and spread it evenly using the bottom of a ladle or tablespoon, then add the funghi trifolati in an even layer.

Add a drizzle of olive oil, then transfer the pizza to the hot stone in the oven and cook for 6 minutes at 240°C (gas mark 9), or for 5 minutes if the oven can reach 250°C (gas mark 10).

Remove the pizza from the oven using the pizza peel. Lay the smoked carrot pancetta evenly on top of the pizza, followed by the mozzarella, then return the pizza to the oven to cook for a further 1 minute.

Once the pizza is ready, take it out of the oven, scatter over the parsley, lemon zest and black pepper to garnish, then finish with another drizzle of olive oil. Serve and enjoy!

Pictured on page 105, number 3.

ASPARAGUS, CHERRY TOMATO AND PARMESAN PIZZA

- WITH CRUSHED HAZELNUTS -

This one flips the traditional pizza formula on its head. Where expert pizza chefs
learn to work with the zesty and biting notes of the San Marzano tomato sauce with
their other toppings, here the sauce is relatively mild, allowing the flavours from
the toppings to truly shine. The sweet, punchy cherry tomatoes combine perfectly
with the deep and rich Parmesan, all with a backdrop of earthy hazelnuts,
which also provide a subtle crunch to the texture.

MAKES 1 PIZZA

semolina flour or rice flour, for dusting
1 dough ball (see pages 12–21)
50g Asparagus Sauce (see page 31)
80g yellow cherry tomatoes, quartered
a pinch of dried sage
extra virgin olive oil, for drizzling
50g Cashew Mozzarella (see page 40)
  or Cashew Buffalo Mozzarella
  (see page 46)

TO FINISH
30g Grated Nut Parmesan (see page 41)
a handful of crushed toasted hazelnuts
a pinch of dried sage

Turn the oven to the highest temperature setting, place a pizza stone on the highest
shelf in the oven and leave it to heat for at least 1 hour (once the oven has reached
full temperature) before baking your pizza.

Generously dust the work surface with flour and flour your hands. Place the dough
ball on the work surface and coat it with flour, then shape it by flattening and
stretching it using your fingers to make your base (you are aiming for a flat base with
slightly thicker, raised edges to make the crust). Pick the pizza base up and gently
stretch it a little further over your fists without tearing it. Brush off any excess flour.

Sprinkle a little flour on the pizza peel and gently place the pizza base onto it. Pour
the asparagus sauce onto the centre of the base and spread it evenly using the
bottom of a ladle or tablespoon, then add the cherry tomatoes in an even layer on
top and sprinkle over the sage. Drizzle over a little olive oil.

Transfer the pizza to the hot stone in the oven and cook for 6 minutes at 240°C
(gas mark 9), or for 5 minutes if the oven can reach 250°C (gas mark 10).

Remove the pizza from the oven using the pizza peel. Spread the mozzarella evenly
over the top, then return the pizza to the oven to cook for a further 1 minute.

Once the pizza is ready, take it out of the oven, then scatter over the grated Parmesan
and crushed hazelnuts. Add another drizzle of olive oil and the sage to finish. Serve
and enjoy!

Pictured on page 104, number 4.

SUN-DRIED TOMATO PESTO AND COURGETTE PIZZA

Sun-dried tomato pesto is a great alternative to the traditional *pesto alla genovese*. It pairs well with any vegetables, in particular with courgettes, bringing to the table a true taste of Sicily, which is where most of the Italian sun-dried tomatoes come from. The ultimate touch is given by the crunchiness of the pistachios, another pillar of Mediterranean cuisine, defined by the Sicilians as the 'green gold' of the island.

MAKES 1 PIZZA

semolina flour or rice flour, for dusting
1 dough ball (see pages 12–21)
80ml Sun-dried Tomato Pesto Sauce
    (see page 27)
50–60g Cashew Mozzarella (see page
    40) or Cashew Buffalo Mozzarella
    (see page 46)

FOR THE COURGETTES

60g courgettes, cut into 5mm-thick
    slices
a pinch of fine pink Himalayan salt
a pinch of freshly ground black pepper

TO FINISH

a small handful of crushed pistachio nuts
a few basil leaves or micro herbs
a pinch of nutritional yeast
a drizzle of extra virgin olive oil
a drizzle of balsamic glaze

Turn the oven to the highest temperature setting, place a pizza stone on the highest shelf in the oven and leave it to heat for at least 1 hour (once the oven has reached full temperature) before baking your pizza.

Prepare the courgettes. Preheat the grill to medium and line the rack in a grill pan with foil. Place the courgette slices in a single layer on the lined grill rack, then grill them for 2 minutes on each side.

Generously dust the work surface with flour and flour your hands. Place the dough ball on the work surface and coat it with flour, then shape it by flattening and stretching it using your fingers to make your base (you are aiming for a flat base with slightly thicker, raised edges to make the crust). Pick the pizza base up and gently stretch it a little further over your fists without tearing it. Brush off any excess flour.

Sprinkle a little flour on the pizza peel and gently place the pizza base onto it. Spoon the pesto sauce onto the centre of the base and spread it evenly using the bottom of a ladle or tablespoon, then top evenly with the grilled courgettes.

Transfer the pizza to the hot stone in the oven and cook for 6 minutes at 240°C (gas mark 9), or for 5 minutes if the oven can reach 250°C (gas mark 10).

Remove the pizza from the oven using the pizza peel. Spread the mozzarella evenly over the top of the pizza, then return it to the oven to cook for a further 1 minute.

Once the pizza is ready, take it out of the oven, scatter over the crushed pistachios, basil leaves or micro herbs and nutritional yeast, followed by a drizzle of olive oil and balsamic glaze to finish. Serve and enjoy!

RED CABBAGE, GRILLED AUBERGINE AND SHIITAKE PIZZA

- WITH FRIED PARSNIPS -

Using a gorgeous red cabbage sauce, which offers a gentle and mildly sweet flavour, this is one of our favourite winter warmers. Grilled aubergine, fried parsnips and shiitake mushrooms make for an amazing combo atop the bright purple sauce. In fact, you may want to add a few extra shiitake mushrooms and parsnips to this recipe – it's almost impossible to avoid snacking on them.

MAKES 1 PIZZA

semolina flour or rice flour, for dusting
1 dough ball (see pages 12–21)
50ml Red Cabbage Sauce (see page 35)
50g Cashew Mozzarella (see page 40)
   or Cashew Buffalo Mozzarella
   (see page 46)

FOR THE AUBERGINES
50g aubergine, cut into 5mm-thick slices
a pinch of fine pink Himalayan salt
a pinch of freshly ground black pepper

FOR THE FRIED PARSNIPS
sunflower oil, for deep-frying
1 small parsnip, peeled and spiralised
   or cut into thin matchstick strips

FOR THE FRIED SHIITAKE MUSHROOMS
50g fresh shiitake mushrooms
50g rice flour or plain flour

TO FINISH
a pinch of chopped parsley
a pinch of dried chilli flakes

Turn the oven to the highest temperature setting, place a pizza stone on the highest shelf in the oven and leave it to heat for at least 1 hour (once the oven has reached full temperature) before baking your pizza.

Prepare the aubergines. Preheat a griddle pan over a high heat. Place the aubergine slices in the pan in a single layer and griddle for 2 minutes on each side. Remove from the heat, season with the salt and black pepper and set aside.

For the parsnips, three-quarters fill a deep pan with sunflower oil (or use a deep-fat fryer) and heat the oil to a temperature of 180°C, (or until a cube of bread browns in 30 seconds). Line a plate with kitchen paper. Add the parsnip to the hot oil and deep-fry for 1 minute, until golden and crispy. Transfer to the lined plate, to drain off the excess oil. Set aside. Heat the oil back to the correct temperature as you'll use this to fry the mushrooms next. Line another plate with kitchen paper.

Wash the shiitake mushrooms, then cut into chunky pieces. Put the flour in a small bowl, then toss the still-wet shiitake pieces in the flour to coat. Brush off the excess flour, then add the mushrooms to the hot oil and deep-fry for 1 minute, until golden and crispy. Transfer to the lined plate, to drain off the excess oil. Set aside.

Generously dust the work surface with flour and flour your hands. Place the dough ball on the work surface and coat it with flour, then shape it by flattening and stretching it using your fingers to make your base (you are aiming for a flat base with slightly thicker, raised edges to make the crust). Pick the pizza base up and gently stretch it a little further over your fists without tearing it. Brush off any excess flour.

Sprinkle a little flour on the pizza peel and gently place the pizza base onto it. Pour the red cabbage sauce onto the centre of the base and spread it evenly using the bottom of a ladle or tablespoon, then lay the aubergines and mushrooms evenly over the top. Transfer the pizza to the hot stone in the oven and cook for 6 minutes at 240°C (gas mark 9), or for 5 minutes if the oven can reach 250°C (gas mark 10).

Remove the pizza from the oven using the pizza peel. Spread the mozzarella in an even layer on top of the pizza, then return it to the oven to cook for a further 1 minute. Once the pizza is ready, take it out of the oven. Scatter over the fried parsnips and garnish with the parsley and chilli flakes. Serve and enjoy!

CHICORY, RICOTTA, OLIVE AND CAPER CALZONE

A calzone is a folded pizza which, just like the classic pizza before it, hails from Naples. Many in Italy will say that the calzone is their favourite form of pizza. It's easier to eat, less messy, and can be stuffed to the brim with delicious ingredients. Here we make a classic calzone by combining stir-fried chicory with a light and delicate ricotta, allowing the naturally salty olives and capers to be the star of the show. To give the calzone an authentic Italian twist, try swapping the chicory for *scarole*, a leafy Italian vegetable similar to kale and spinach, with a delicate texture and rich flavour.

MAKES 1 PIZZA

sunflower oil, for deep-frying
semolina flour or rice flour, for dusting
½ dough ball (see pages 12-21)
30g Stir-fried Chicory with Capers,
 Garlic and Olives (see page 60)
30g Almond Ricotta (see page 45)
3-4 pitted black olives, halved
3 capers, drained
a pinch of freshly ground black pepper

Three-quarters fill a deep pan with sunflower oil (or use a deep-fat fryer) and heat the oil to a temperature of 180°C, (or until a cube of bread browns in 30 seconds).

Generously dust the work surface with flour and flour your hands. Place the half dough ball on the work surface and coat it with flour, then shape it by flattening and stretching it using your fingers to make your base (you are aiming for an even thickness of 2-3mm - you need to ensure it's not too thin, especially in the middle). Pick the pizza base up and brush off any excess flour.

Sprinkle some more flour onto the work surface and then gently place the disc of dough on to it. Spoon the chicory mixture onto the centre of the dough, followed by the ricotta, olives, capers and black pepper.

Fold one half of the dough over the top of the filling to make a semi-circular shape, ensuring the edges meet and match the opposite side. Press the edges together with your fingertips to seal them together tightly.

Carefully place the calzone into the hot oil, frying it for about 30 seconds on each side until cooked and golden. Remove the calzone and place it on a kitchen paper-lined plate to remove the excess oil from both sides, then serve.

PEAR, GORGONZOLA AND WALNUT PIZZA

- WITH BALSAMIC GLAZE -

The Italian grandmas always say *'Al contadino non far sapere, quant'è buono il cacio con le pere'*, which means 'don't let the farmer know how good cheese is with pears'. If the farmers knew, they would have probably kept all the cheese and pears for themselves! This age-old saying perfectly describes how good this combination really is. The sweetness of the pears and punchy taste of the Gorgonzola make a perfectly balanced pizza, which, when topped with walnuts and balsamic glaze, becomes a rustic explosion of flavours.

MAKES 1 PIZZA

semolina flour or rice flour, for dusting
1 dough ball (see pages 12-21)
extra virgin olive oil, for drizzling
60-70g Almond Gorgonzola Cheese
  (see page 41)

FOR THE PEAR

100g peeled and cored ripe pears
  (prepared weight), cut into
  5mm-thick slices
1 tablespoon agave syrup
¼ teaspoon ground cinnamon
a pinch of fine pink Himalayan salt
a pinch of freshly ground black pepper

TO FINISH

a small handful of crushed walnuts
a drizzle of balsamic glaze

Turn the oven to the highest temperature setting, place a pizza stone on the highest shelf in the oven and leave it to heat for at least 1 hour (once the oven has reached full temperature) before baking your pizza.

Prepare the pear. In a bowl, mix the pear slices with the rest of the ingredients and leave them to marinate for 10 minutes.

Generously dust the work surface with flour and flour your hands. Place the dough ball on the work surface and coat it with flour, then shape it by flattening and stretching it using your fingers to make your base (you are aiming for a flat base with slightly thicker, raised edges to make the crust). Pick the pizza base up and gently stretch it a little further over your fists without tearing it. Brush off any excess flour.

Sprinkle a little flour on the pizza peel and gently place the pizza base onto it. Drizzle a little olive oil onto the pizza base, then arrange the marinated pear slices evenly over the top.

Transfer the pizza to the hot stone in the oven and cook for 6 minutes at 240°C (gas mark 9), or for 5 minutes if the oven can reach 250°C (gas mark 10).

Remove the pizza from the oven using the pizza peel. Place the Gorgonzola evenly on top of the pizza, then return it to the oven to cook for a further 1 minute.

Once the pizza is ready, take it out of the oven, scatter over the crushed walnuts, drizzle over some balsamic glaze and finish with a drizzle of olive oil. Serve and enjoy!

CARROT PARMA HAM, CHERRY TOMATO AND ROCKET PIZZA

The region of Parma is famed for its ham as well as its cheese. The eponymous Parma ham spends 1–3 years in preparation here, whilst Parmesan cheese takes at least 12 months to develop and ferment. Luckily, when you do things the plant-based way, you don't have to wait all that long. Our plant-based Parmesan and Parma ham will be ready quickly, and this pizza is an ode to the Parma region, combining both with cherry tomatoes and rocket.

MAKES 1 PIZZA

semolina flour or rice flour, for dusting
1 dough ball (see pages 12–21)
40g cherry or baby plum tomatoes, quartered
extra virgin olive oil, for drizzling
a pinch of fine pink Himalayan salt
6 basil leaves
50g Cashew Mozzarella (see page 40) or Cashew Buffalo Mozzarella (see page 46)
4–5 slices Carrot Parma Ham (see page 66)

TO FINISH
a handful of rocket leaves
20g Grated Nut Parmesan (see page 41)

Turn the oven to the highest temperature setting, place a pizza stone on the highest shelf in the oven and leave it to heat for at least 1 hour (once the oven has reached full temperature) before baking your pizza.

Generously dust the work surface with flour and flour your hands. Place the dough ball on the work surface and coat it with flour, then shape it by flattening and stretching it using your fingers to make your base (you are aiming for a flat base with slightly thicker, raised edges to make the crust). Pick the pizza base up and gently stretch it a little further over your fists without tearing it. Brush off any excess flour.

Sprinkle a little flour on the pizza peel and gently place the pizza base onto it. Top the base evenly with the cherry or baby plum tomatoes, then add a drizzle of olive oil and the salt.

Transfer the pizza to the hot stone in the oven and cook for 6 minutes at 240°C (gas mark 9), or for 5 minutes if the oven can reach 250°C (gas mark 10).

Remove the pizza from the oven using the pizza peel. Scatter the basil leaves over the pizza, spread the mozzarella evenly on top, followed by the Parma ham slices. Return the pizza to the oven to cook for a further 1 minute.

Once the pizza is ready, take it out of the oven. Scatter the rocket leaves over, followed by the Parmesan, then finish with a drizzle of olive oil. Serve and enjoy!

Pictured on page 119, number 1.

ARTICHOKE AND PECORINO PIZZA

Pecorino has a much richer, deeper and sharper flavour profile than other cheeses, and thus on this pizza we let it be the star of the show. By balancing it with the mild flavoured but textured artichoke, we can allow the cashew and walnut pecorino to truly sing of its own accord. This is our favourite way to enjoy this wonderful plant-based cheese.

MAKES 1 PIZZA

semolina flour or rice flour, for dusting
1 dough ball (see pages 12–21)
50g San Marzano Plum Tomato and Basil 'Passata' Sauce (see page 24)
60g artichoke heart quarters from a jar, drained
a few basil leaves
50g Cashew Mozzarella (see page 40) or Cashew Buffalo Mozzarella (see page 46)
50g Cashew and Walnut Pecorino (see page 44), grated
a drizzle of extra virgin olive oil

Turn the oven to the highest temperature setting, place a pizza stone on the highest shelf in the oven and leave it to heat for at least 1 hour (once the oven has reached full temperature) before baking your pizza.

Generously dust the work surface with flour and flour your hands. Place the dough ball on the work surface and coat it with flour, then shape it by flattening and stretching it using your fingers to make your base (you are aiming for a flat base with slightly thicker, raised edges to make the crust). Pick the pizza base up and gently stretch it a little further over your fists without tearing it. Brush off any excess flour.

Sprinkle a little flour on the pizza peel and gently place the pizza base onto it. Pour the tomato sauce onto the centre of the base and spread it evenly using the bottom of a ladle or tablespoon. Add the artichoke quarters to the pizza base in an even layer.

Transfer the pizza to the hot stone in the oven and cook for 6 minutes at 240°C (gas mark 9), or for 5 minutes if the oven can reach 250°C (gas mark 10).

Remove the pizza from the oven using the pizza peel. Scatter the basil leaves over the pizza and spread the mozzarella evenly on top, followed by the pecorino. Return it to the oven to cook for a further 1 minute.

Once the pizza is ready, take it out of the oven. Add a drizzle of olive oil, then serve and enjoy!

Pictured on page 119, number 2.

THREE PEPPER PIZZA

- WITH OLIVES AND CAPERS -

Some of our favourite Mediterranean vegetables form an unstoppable and moreish flavour force here. The mild sweetness of the peppers paired with the intense saltiness of the olives and capers creates a natural umami-style taste sensation that ticks all of the right boxes. Peppers, capers and olives have been natural partners in Italian cuisine for a long time, and it's not hard to see why.

MAKES 1 PIZZA

semolina flour or rice flour, for dusting
1 dough ball (see pages 12-21)
50g San Marzano Plum Tomato and Basil 'Passata' Sauce (see page 24)
70g Pan-fried Peppers with Garlic Sauce (see page 62)
8-9 pitted black olives, left whole
5-6 capers, drained
50g Cashew Mozzarella (see page 40) or Cashew Buffalo Mozzarella (see page 46)

TO FINISH
a few basil leaves
a pinch of nutritional yeast
a drizzle of extra virgin olive oil

Turn the oven to the highest temperature setting, place a pizza stone on the highest shelf in the oven and leave it to heat for at least 1 hour (once the oven has reached full temperature) before baking your pizza.

Generously dust the work surface with flour and flour your hands. Place the dough ball on the work surface and coat it with flour, then shape it by flattening and stretching it using your fingers to make your base (you are aiming for a flat base with slightly thicker, raised edges to make the crust). Pick the pizza base up and gently stretch it a little further over your fists without tearing it. Brush off any excess flour.

Sprinkle a little flour on the pizza peel and gently place the pizza base onto it. Pour the tomato sauce onto the centre of the base and spread it evenly using the bottom of a ladle or tablespoon. Spoon the peppers evenly over the top and then scatter over the olives and capers.

Transfer the pizza to the hot stone in the oven and cook for 6 minutes at 240°C (gas mark 9), or for 5 minutes if the oven can reach 250°C (gas mark 10).

Remove the pizza from the oven using the pizza peel. Spread the mozzarella evenly on top, then return the pizza to the oven to cook for a further 1 minute.

Once the pizza is ready, take it out of the oven, add a few basil leaves, scatter over the nutritional yeast and finish with a drizzle of olive oil. Enjoy!

Pictured on page 119, number 3.

GLUTEN-FREE TUNA-STYLE AND YELLOW BABY TOMATO FOCACCIA

We've never met anyone who doesn't love focaccia, so here's the ultimate recipe to wow them. Using baby plum tomatoes, but also our tomato-based 'tuna', this has a subtle flavour of the ocean. It's finished with some of our plant-based spreadable cheese sauce, which is buttery smooth and incredibly creamy. Be sure to give yourself time to prepare the plant-based tuna-style recipe, because it's so worth it for this delicious bread.

MAKES 1 FOCACCIA/SERVES 4 (OR SERVES MORE AS FINGER FOOD)

extra virgin olive oil, for drizzling
1 gluten-free dough ball (see pages 19–21)
60g Spreadable Cheese with Capers and Chives (see page 45)
10 pieces of Tuna-style Plum Tomatoes (see page 67)

FOR THE BABY TOMATOES
50g yellow baby plum or cherry tomatoes, halved
½ garlic clove, finely chopped
a drizzle of extra virgin olive oil
3 basil leaves, chopped
a pinch of salt

TO FINISH
a few basil leaves
a pinch of freshly ground black pepper

Prepare the baby tomatoes. Place all the ingredients in a small bowl and gently mix together, then set aside for later.

Take a 23cm square or round (3cm deep) non-stick baking tray, drizzle in plenty of olive oil and use your hand to spread it over the bottom and sides of the tray. Set aside.

Unwrap the dough ball and flip it onto your oiled hand. Lay it in the middle of the prepared baking tray, then starting from the middle of the dough ball, gently flatten and stretch it using your fingers to create an even thickness, shaping the dough so that it covers the bottom of the tray completely, working it into the corners.

When the dough is completely stretched, make many deep indentations in the surface of the dough, pushing your fingertips into the dough so you almost touch the bottom of the tray each time. Drizzle a generous amount of olive oil over the dough, spreading it over the entire surface using a silicone brush. Cover the tray with a clean tea towel and leave to rest in a warm place for 45–60 minutes, until the dough has risen.

Meanwhile, turn the oven to the highest temperature setting and leave it to preheat for at least 25–30 minutes (to reach full temperature) before baking your focaccia.

Uncover, then transfer the focaccia to the middle shelf in the oven and cook for 20 minutes at 240°C (gas mark 9), or for 18 minutes if the oven can reach 250°C (gas mark 10), or until golden.

Remove from the oven, then carefully remove the focaccia from the tin and transfer it to a wire rack. Leave to cool for 20 minutes.

After 20 minutes, pour the cheese sauce onto the centre of the focaccia and spread evenly using the bottom of a spoon. Top the focaccia evenly with the yellow tomatoes and tuna-style tomato pieces, then finish with a few basil leaves and the black pepper. Cut into four, or cut into smaller portions and serve as finger food.

Pictured on page 118, number 4.

PASTA

Whilst it's rare for us to want something other than pizza, on those occasions when we do, pasta is our favourite alternative. We've loved playing our part in creating plant-based options in Italian cuisine and couldn't resist turning our attention to pasta. This selection of recipes includes our take on dishes that are routinely packed with cream, cheese and meat.

CASHEW NUT
AND LEMON LINGUINE

- WITH SPRING VEGETABLES -

Linguine is a type of pasta similar to spaghetti, but flat. It originated in Genoa and has traditionally accompanied dishes with a creamy sauce. The buttery taste of cashew nuts marries well with linguine, creating a delicate pasta alternative to the more common spaghetti. Lemon adds a fresh flavour to the dish, which can be enjoyed at any time of the year, although here it's presented with spring vegetables.

SERVES 2

FOR THE CASHEW CREAM
180g blanched unsalted cashew nuts
3 tablespoons freshly squeezed lemon juice
1 tablespoon finely grated lemon zest
2 tablespoons nutritional yeast
1 teaspoon fine pink Himalayan salt
¼ teaspoon freshly ground pepper, plus extra (optional) to serve
240ml any plant-based milk (but avoid coconut milk)

FOR THE VEGETABLES AND PASTA
1 tablespoon fine pink Himalayan salt, plus 3 pinches
4 fine asparagus spears
2½ tablespoons extra virgin olive oil, plus an extra drizzle
squeeze of lemon juice
2 shallots, finely chopped
130g frozen green peas
200g dried linguine (gluten-free alternatives can also be used)

Prepare the cashew cream. Add all the ingredients to a high-speed blender and blend until the mixture becomes combined and creamy, scraping down the sides once or twice, if necessary. Set aside.

Prepare the vegetables and pasta. Bring a deep saucepan of water to the boil and add a pinch of salt. Trim the asparagus, then add it to the pan, upright, and cook it for 8 minutes until tender. Drain, place the asparagus into a bowl of cold water with another pinch of salt and let it cool. Once cool, drain, place the spears in a dish and drizzle over a little olive oil and the squeeze of lemon. Set aside to marinate whilst you prepare the peas.

Heat the measured olive oil in a pan over a medium heat, add the shallots and cook for 30 seconds. Add the peas and the remaining pinch of salt and cook for 8 minutes, stirring occasionally.

Meanwhile, half-fill a deep pot with water, add the remaining 1 tablespoon of salt, then bring the water to the boil. Add the linguine and cook for 10 minutes (or according to the packet instructions) until al dente.

In the meantime, add the cashew cream to the peas in the pan along with a splash of water, and cook them together over a low heat for about 3 minutes. Once the linguine is ready, drain it, then add it to the creamy peas and gently mix them together using spaghetti tongs.

Divide the linguine mixture between two plates and serve with the asparagus spears on top and an extra sprinkle of black pepper, if you like.

SPAGHETTI WITH SUN-DRIED TOMATOES, CAPERS, TAPENADE AND ALMONDS

The only thing missing from this recipe is a genuine Italian mamma and a little fresh Tuscan countryside air. This takes a few of our absolute favourite Italian flavours, such as punchy sun-dried tomatoes and salty capers, and combines them with classic spaghetti. This is everything a true Italian pasta lover adores, together in one dish. Perfect in the height of summer, served with a good Chianti.

SERVES 2

2 tablespoons extra virgin olive oil
4 tablespoons Tapenade (see page 79)
½ teaspoon capers, drained
60g sun-dried tomatoes in oil, drained, patted dry and chopped into 1cm-thick slices
a pinch of chopped parsley
1 tablespoon fine pink Himalayan salt
180g dried spaghetti (gluten-free alternatives can also be used)

TO GARNISH

2 teaspoons crushed unsalted blanched almonds
1-2 pinches of chopped parsley
1-2 pinches of freshly ground black pepper

Heat the olive oil in a frying pan over a medium heat, then add the tapenade and capers and cook for 2 minutes, stirring occasionally. Add the sun-dried tomatoes and parsley and stir for a further 1 minute. Turn off the heat and set aside for later.

Half-fill a deep pot with water, add the salt and bring to the boil. Add the spaghetti and cook for 10 minutes (or according to the packet instructions) until al dente.

Meanwhile, after the pasta has been cooking for a few minutes, using a ladle, take some cooking water (about ½ ladleful) and pour it into the pan containing the sun-dried tomato mixture, stirring to mix. A minute or so before the pasta is ready, turn on the heat to low under the sauce.

Once the spaghetti is ready, drain it, then add it to the sun-dried tomato mixture and gently mix them together using spaghetti tongs.

Divide the spaghetti mixture between two serving plates, sprinkle the crushed almonds and chopped parsley over to garnish, then finish with a little black pepper. Enjoy!

PENNE ALLA NORMA

- TOMATO AND AUBERGINE SAUCE WITH PECORINO -

Penne alla Norma shows off the very best of Sicilian cuisine in a single dish. Whilst undeniably Italian, Sicily's position to the south of Italy has provided it with a wider number of cultural influences, including Greek, French and Arabic cuisines. You get a sense of this from the addition of aubergine and grated pecorino featured in the dish, whilst the core ingredients and flavours remain distinctly Italian.

SERVES 2

250g aubergine (1 large aubergine)
1 tablespoon fine pink Himalayan salt,
   plus extra for salting the aubergines,
   and an extra pinch
150ml sunflower oil, for frying
2 tablespoons extra virgin olive oil
1 garlic clove, finely chopped
300g large tomatoes or Roma plum
   tomatoes, cut into chunky pieces
10 basil leaves, torn or chopped into
   small pieces
180g dried penne (gluten-free
   alternatives can also be used)

TO GARNISH
2 tablespoons Cashew and Walnut
   Pecorino (see page 44), grated
6 fried aubergine strips (see method)

Cut the aubergine into 1cm chunks (also cutting six strips to make the garnish), putting the chunks (and strips) into a colander as you go and sprinkling them with plenty of salt. The salt will help the aubergine to dry out, so once all the chunks (and strips) are salted, leave them to sit (over a sink or bowl) for at least 30 minutes.

Take whole handfuls of the salted aubergine chunks (and strips), lay them on kitchen paper, then wrap them up in the paper and squeeze out any excess water. Drop the dried aubergines into a large bowl and repeat with the remaining aubergine chunks.

Heat the sunflower oil in a pan over a medium heat until hot. Add the aubergine and fry until it begins to crisp and brown around the edges, turning it occasionally. The aubergine should be tender but still have a good structure. Lay the fried aubergine chunks (and strips) out on a baking sheet lined with kitchen paper to absorb any excess oil. Set the strips aside for the garnish.

Heat the olive oil in a large pan over a low heat and add the garlic. After about 30 seconds, add the tomatoes and five or six of the chopped basil leaves. Sauté over a very brisk heat, stirring often, until the tomatoes begin to resemble a chunky sauce.

Carefully add the aubergine (apart from the aubergine strips) to the tomato mixture - the aubergine will be very tender at this point. Stir in a pinch of salt, then turn off the heat and set aside for later.

Half-fill a deep pot with water, add the remaining 1 tablespoon of salt, and bring the water to the boil. Add the penne and cook for 10 minutes (or according to the packet instructions) until al dente. After the pasta has been cooking for a few minutes, using a ladle, take some cooking water (about ½ ladleful) and pour it into the pan containing the tomato/aubergine mixture, stirring to mix. A minute or so before the pasta is ready, turn on the heat to low under the sauce.

Once the penne is ready, drain it in a colander, then add it to the tomato/aubergine sauce and gently mix them together using a wooden spoon.

Divide the penne mixture between two serving plates, sprinkle the grated pecorino over to garnish, top with the reserved fried aubergine strips and finish with the remaining basil. Enjoy!

BEETROOT AND PROSECCO RISOTTO

- WITH CHIVE CREAM -

Italy is famous for pasta, pizza and risotto. The type of rice traditionally used for making a perfect risotto is called Arborio rice, an Italian short-grain rice cultivated in North Italy, famous for its creamy texture. Combining beetroots with the delicate taste of Arborio rice and a couple of dashes of Prosecco, gives this traditional Italian dish a new, exciting flavour.

SERVES 2

FOR THE CHIVE CREAM
180g unsalted blanched cashew nuts
2 tablespoons nutritional yeast
30g chopped chives (fresh or dried)
1 teaspoon fine pink Himalayan salt

FOR THE RISOTTO
800ml boiling water
½ vegetable stock cube
a drizzle of extra virgin olive oil
1 small red onion
150g raw beetroots, peeled and cut
   into small cubes
200g Arborio rice
3 tablespoons vegan Prosecco
1 teaspoon fine pink Himalayan salt

Prepare the chive cream. Put all the chive cream ingredients into a high-speed blender with 240ml of water and blend together until the mixture becomes smooth and creamy, scraping down the sides once or twice, if necessary. Set aside.

Prepare the risotto. For the stock, pour the boiling water into a small pan, crumble in the stock cube and bring back to a gentle simmer. Keep it gently simmering over a low heat.

Heat the olive oil in a pan over a medium heat, add the red onion and sweat for 30 seconds. Stir in the beetroot and cook for about 4 minutes until soft, stirring occasionally. Add the rice to the pan and cook it over a low heat for 1–2 minutes. Add the Prosecco and stir for 2–3 minutes, until it has reduced.

Gradually add the hot stock (about 200ml at a time), stirring continuously over a medium heat, allowing each addition of stock to be absorbed before adding the next. It should take about 15-18 minutes for all the stock to be added and absorbed, and by this stage the risotto should be al dente and creamy. Stir in the salt.

To serve, divide the risotto between two serving plates, and top each portion with a generous drizzle of the chive cream.

Tip Store any leftover chive cream in an airtight container in the fridge for up to 3 days. It can be served with crackers.

TAGLIATELLE WITH WILD MUSHROOMS AND ASPARAGUS SAUCE

The origins of tagliatelle are legendary, almost that of a fairytale – rumour has it that a talented court chef invented the dish to honour Lucrezia Borgia's marriage to Duke Alfonso D'Este in 1487. Whilst we can't lend credence to the tale, this dish is almost the stuff of fairytales itself. The silky smooth asparagus sauce pairs perfectly with the earthy notes of wild mushrooms. A feast that's truly fit for an Italian princess.

SERVES 2

2 tablespoons extra virgin olive oil
4 tablespoons Asparagus Sauce
  (see page 31)
150g Funghi Trifolati (see page 54)
a pinch of chopped fresh parsley
1 tablespoon fine pink Himalayan salt
180g dried tagliatelle (gluten-free
  alternatives can also be used)

TO GARNISH
2 tablespoons crushed walnuts
1 teaspoon nutritional yeast
2 teaspoons chopped parsley
1-2 pinches of freshly ground black
  pepper

Heat the olive oil in a frying pan over a medium heat. Add the asparagus sauce and cook for 2 minutes, stirring occasionally. Add the mushrooms (reserve a few pieces for the garnish) and parsley and stir for a further minute. Turn off the heat and set aside for later.

Half-fill a deep pot with water, add the remaining 1 tablespoon of salt, then bring to the boil. Add the tagliatelle and cook for 10 minutes (or according to the packet instructions) until al dente.

Meanwhile, after the pasta has been cooking for a few minutes, using a ladle, take some cooking water (about ½ ladleful) and pour it into the pan containing the asparagus and mushroom mixture, stirring to mix. A minute or so before the pasta is ready, turn on the heat to low under the sauce.

Once the tagliatelle is ready, drain it, then add it to the asparagus and mushroom sauce and gently mix them together using spaghetti tongs.

Divide the tagliatelle mixture between two serving plates, combine the crushed walnuts and nutritional yeast and sprinkle this over the pasta to garnish. Scatter over the parsley, top with the reserved mushrooms, then finish with a little black pepper. Enjoy!

LASAGNE WITH MUSHROOM RAGÙ AND BÉCHAMEL

Whether you're vegan or not, this is one of those dishes that will amaze you. The mushroom-based ragù is indistinguishable from beef, and the coating of creamy Béchamel sauce makes this lasagne excellent comfort food, and a simple yet delicious dish to serve to big groups and families – it's easy to scale up the recipe to serve more. This one typically makes its way into our dinner rotation at least once a fortnight, and we continue to look forward to it every single time.

SERVES 2

6 dried lasagne sheets (gluten-free alternatives can also be used)
nutritional yeast, for sprinkling

FOR THE RAGÙ

2 tablespoons extra virgin olive oil
½ carrot, peeled and finely chopped
½ celery stick, finely chopped
¼ red onion, finely chopped
1 garlic clove, finely chopped
150g fresh shiitake mushrooms, finely chopped
1 tablespoon coconut aminos
1 tablespoon vegan red wine
300g Regular Tomato Sauce (see page 25)
½ sprig of rosemary
½ teaspoon fine pink Himalayan salt
a pinch of freshly ground black pepper
10 basil leaves

FOR THE BÉCHAMEL SAUCE

400ml any plant-based milk (but avoid coconut milk)
½ small onion
2 cloves
½ teaspoon fine pink Himalayan salt
20g cornflour
40ml sunflower oil
1 teaspoon nutritional yeast
a pinch of freshly grated nutmeg
a pinch of freshly ground black pepper

Prepare the ragù. Heat the olive oil in a pan, add the carrot, celery, onion and garlic (this finely chopped mixture of veg is known as the 'soffritto') and fry for about 1 minute until soft, stirring occasionally. Add the mushrooms, then stir in the coconut aminos and red wine. Add the tomato sauce, rosemary sprig, salt and black pepper and stir to mix. Cover and cook over a low heat for 3 hours, stirring occasionally. Once cooked, remove the rosemary stalk and stir in the basil.

When the ragù is almost cooked, preheat the oven to 180°C (gas mark 4) and prepare the Béchamel sauce. Put the milk in a pan, add the onion, cloves and salt and bring gently to the boil. Meanwhile, mix the cornflour with the sunflower oil, nutritional yeast and nutmeg in a small bowl. When the milk is boiling, take out the onion and cloves and add the flour and oil mixture and black pepper. Stir continuously with a whisk over a low heat until the sauce thickens.

To assemble as two individual lasagne, take two individual lasagne dishes (about 15 x 10cm) and place a spoonful of the ragù in the bottom of each. Place one lasagne sheet on top (cut to fit the dishes, if necessary). Add another spoonful of ragù on top, then a spoonful of Béchamel sauce, followed by a sprinkling of nutritional yeast. Repeat these layers, then finish with a sheet of lasagne (you will have used three sheets of lasagne in each dish). Top the lasagne sheets with the remaining ragù, then the remaining Béchamel sauce and a final sprinkle of nutritional yeast. If you're using a larger 30 x 30cm oven dish, follow the steps as above but using two spoonfuls of sauce and two lasagne sheets for each layer.

Bake the lasagne in the oven for 20 minutes, until golden. Serve immediately.

DESSERTS

Finally, it's time to satisfy the sweet tooth. Italian desserts are known for being chock-full of dairy... namely cream, cream and more cream. Rather than seeing this as insurmountable, we saw it as an exciting challenge, and over the years have developed a repertoire of delicious desserts, designed around classic Italian cuisine. By understanding the flavour and texture of cream, we can understand how to mimic it. The secret is plant-based fats such as nuts and coconut. The great thing is you lose nothing when it comes to flavour and texture, and yet the resulting dish is significantly better for you than those using dairy cream.

GLUTEN-FREE TIRAMISÙ

Tiramisù is undoubtedly the most popular Italian dessert. The word tiramisù means
'cheer me up', and this plant-based version of the traditional dish does exactly
that! Aquafaba is a perfect egg replacer and it is used in a variety of desserts.
Combined with apple cider vinegar, it makes a delicious cream alternative that
marries well with the strong flavour of coffee, usually found in tiramisù.
We recommend serving the tiramisù in two medium-sized cylindrical glasses
to create individual desserts.

SERVES 2

FOR THE CREAM
240g coconut cream (from a can of
full-fat coconut milk)
4 tablespoons aquafaba (this is the
water from a can of chickpeas)
1 tablespoon soft brown sugar
¼ teaspoon apple cider vinegar
1 teaspoon vanilla paste or 2 teaspoons
vanilla extract

FOR THE SPONGE CAKE
2 tablespoons sunflower oil, plus extra
for greasing
240g gluten-free plain flour
1 teaspoon baking powder
120g soft brown sugar
a pinch of fine pink Himalayan salt
300ml rice milk
1 teaspoon apple cider vinegar
or lemon juice
1 teaspoon vanilla paste or 2 teaspoons
vanilla extract

TO ASSEMBLE AND FINISH
240ml cold espresso coffee
(or brewed cold instant coffee)
raw cocoa powder, for sprinkling

Prepare the cream. Place the coconut cream in the fridge and wait 1 hour before using
it. Once the cream is chilled, transfer it to a bowl and whisk until smooth. Set aside.

In a separate bowl, whip the aquafaba, sugar, vinegar and vanilla paste or extract
together using a handheld electric whisk (or a stand mixer) until it forms stiff peaks
(turn the bowl upside-down to see if the whipped aquafaba slides down; if it does,
keep whipping until it no longer does). It takes 3-5 minutes for the aquafaba to be
whipped properly. With the whisk running on a low speed, gradually add the coconut
cream and whisk for 1 minute. Cover the bowl and refrigerate for 1-2 hours to allow
the cream to set before assembling the tiramisù.

Meanwhile, prepare the sponge cake. Preheat the oven to 190°C (gas mark 5).
Lightly grease a 20 x 20cm baking or cake tin with sunflower oil.

Sift the flour and baking powder into a bowl to remove any lumps. Stir in the sugar
and salt. In another bowl, mix together all the remaining (wet) ingredients using
a spoon, then add this to the flour mixture. Whisk the mixture until smooth and
combined, then pour it into the prepared tin and spread evenly. Bake in the oven
for 30 minutes or until golden brown and cooked through.

Remove from the oven. Cool the cake in the tin for a few minutes, then turn it out
onto a wire rack and leave to cool completely.

Take two medium-sized cylindrical serving glasses. Cut the sponge cake into rounds,
using the top of the glass as your cutter. You will need two round slices of sponge
cake for each glass (any leftover sponge can be enjoyed on its own).

For each dessert, dip a round of sponge into the cold coffee for 3-4 seconds. Place
the sponge at the bottom of a glass and spread some of the cream on top using a
spoon. Repeat to create a couple more layers (or more as you wish), then simply
finish each dessert with a sprinkling of cocoa powder over the top.

Transfer the assembled tiramisù glasses to the fridge and leave to set for 2-3 hours.
Just before serving, sprinkle a little more cocoa powder on top.

CUSTARD CREAM DOUGH BALLS

Italy may not have invented the doughnut, but we put our own delicious twist on it. The *bombolone* is the Italian doughnut. It gets its name from the word 'bomba' meaning 'bomb', because these are usually stuffed to bursting with delicious ingredients, and will typically explode as you bite into each one, leaving you grinning with a mouth covered in custard cream. If that sounds like your idea of heaven, this recipe is most definitely for you.

SERVES 4
(3 DOUGH BALLS PER SERVING)

plain flour, for dusting
2 dough balls (see pages 12–21)

FOR THE CREAM
250ml any sweetened plant-based milk
   (but avoid coconut milk)
45g soft brown sugar
½ teaspoon vanilla extract
finely grated zest of ½ lemon
20g cornflour
a pinch of ground turmeric

TO SERVE
icing sugar, for sprinkling
handful of fresh strawberries, sliced

Prepare the cream. Pour the milk and sugar into a saucepan set over a low heat, then add the vanilla and sprinkle in the lemon zest. Sift the cornflour into the pan, and then begin whisking the mixture until it is smooth. Keep heating the mixture over a low heat, whisking continuously, and as soon as you see it begin to thicken, remove the pan from the heat. Stir in the turmeric to give it a subtle yellow colouring. Allow the mixture to cool, then transfer it to a disposable piping bag.

Meanwhile, prepare the dough balls. Preheat the oven to its highest setting at least 25–30 minutes before baking your dough balls. Line a baking sheet with non-stick baking paper and set aside.

Generously dust the work surface with flour and flour your hands. Place a dough ball on the work surface and coat it with flour, then shape it by flattening and stretching it using your fingers, until it is flat and a uniform thickness (no thicker edges) to make your base. Pick the dough up and lay it on the work surface dusted with a little more flour. Keep stretching it by hand or with a roller to create a 15 x 25cm rectangle which is 2mm thick. With a pizza slicer, divide it in half lengthways and then divide it into three widthways to make six squares of dough. Set these aside. Repeat with the second dough ball to make 12 square pieces of dough in total.

Take the piping bag of cream and snip off the tip of the bag. Pipe a blob of the cream mixture onto the centre of each piece of dough, keeping the blobs an equal size.

One at a time, fold one half of the dough over the top of the cream filling to meet the other side and press the edges together with your fingertips, ensuring the edge is tightly sealed. Take the two ends and join them together by pressing the dough and shaping it into a ball. Repeat until all the dough balls are assembled.

Place the dough balls on the prepared baking sheet, leaving a little space between each one. Bake in the oven for 6 minutes at 240°C (gas mark 9), or for 5 minutes if the oven can reach 250°C (gas mark 10) until cooked and golden brown. Remove from the oven.

Place three hot dough balls on each serving plate, sift a little icing sugar over them, then add some strawberry slices to each plate and serve.

BANOFFEE GELATO

Incredibly simple to make, this dessert is packed with health benefits, and it's easy to store. We almost constantly have this available in the freezer at home, and we serve it in the restaurants. It works great as a dessert on its own, but why not pair it with one of the other desserts in this book for that perfect after-dinner combo? You can have this prepped and in the freezer in minutes, so even if you haven't got time to spare, get this one ready and enjoy a sumptuous dessert later.

SERVES 4

FOR THE GELATO
4 large ripened bananas, peeled, sliced
    and frozen overnight
100ml sweetened almond milk
1 tablespoon agave syrup
30g crushed walnuts

FOR THE 'TOFFEE' SAUCE
120g pitted dates
juice of ½ lemon
1 teaspoon vanilla extract
1 tablespoon flavourless coconut oil
100ml sweetened almond milk

TO SERVE
sliced fresh banana
a small handful of chopped walnuts
vegan chocolate sauce or vegan
    caramel sauce

Prepare the gelato base. Put the frozen bananas and almond milk in a blender or food processor and blend together until combined and smooth in texture. Add the agave syrup and blend again. Pour into a plastic, freezer-proof container with a lid and set aside for now.

Prepare the toffee sauce. Place the dates in a blender or food processor with the lemon juice, vanilla extract, coconut oil and almond milk and whizz together until smooth (scraping down the sides once or twice, if necessary). This will take around 5-10 minutes on a high speed. Depending on how you like your sauce, add a little more milk for a runnier consistency, if desired.

Add the crushed walnuts to the gelato mixture, mixing them together using a spatula. Drizzle over the toffee sauce and fold just a few times to create lovely streaks of toffee throughout. Cover with the lid, then freeze for at least 6 hours or overnight before scooping and serving.

Serve two or three scoops of the gelato in each serving glass or cup. Add a few slices of banana and some chopped walnuts to each serving and finish with a drizzle of vegan chocolate sauce or vegan caramel sauce. Enjoy!

CHOCOLATE FINGERS

– WITH COCONUT SUGAR AND CHOCOLATE SAUCE (SCUGNIZZIELLI) –

Scugnizzielli Napoletani are one of Naples' most famed desserts. For those that have never tried them, picture churros but made with high-quality sourdough. Interested? We thought so. We serve these up with a wickedly indulgent chocolate-coconut sauce, but you can always get creative with how you serve them. They are easy to make, and with a communal dipping sauce, they make for a fantastic dessert for any occasion, be it a family dinner or a large party.

SERVES 4

FOR THE CHOCOLATE SAUCE
2 tablespoons coconut oil
4 tablespoons any sweetened plant-based milk
4 tablespoons maple syrup
25g raw cocoa powder

FOR THE FRIED DOUGH STRIPS
sunflower oil, for deep-frying
200g coconut sugar or soft brown sugar
plain flour, for dusting
2 dough balls (see pages 12-21)

TO SERVE
vegan whipped cream or vegan single cream (optional)

Prepare the chocolate sauce. Melt the coconut oil in a saucepan over a low heat, then stir in the milk and maple syrup. Bring to a very gentle simmer, stirring. Slowly whisk in the cocoa powder and continue to cook over a low heat for about 3 minutes, then remove from the heat. Your sauce is now ready to use. Allow this to cool - it will keep in an airtight container in the fridge for up to a few weeks.

For the dough strips, put enough sunflower oil in a deep pan to three-quarters fill it (or use a deep-fat fryer) and heat the oil to a temperature of 180°C (or until a cube of bread browns in 30 seconds).

Lay some kitchen paper on a plate for later (you'll need this to remove excess oil). Place the coconut or brown sugar in a bowl and set aside.

Generously dust part of the work surface with flour and flour your hands. Place a dough ball on the work surface and coat it with flour, then move the dough to an un-floured surface. Pull the dough at two opposite ends, stretching and flattening it with your fingers to make a rectangle about 15 x 10cm in size and about 2cm thick. With a pizza slicer, cut it in half widthways and then cut each half into four equal strips lengthways. Repeat with the second ball of dough.

Pick up the dough strips and brush off any excess flour, gently pull the strips at each end, and then add them, one at a time, to the hot oil. Deep-fry each strip for about 30 seconds on each side, until cooked and golden, then use a skimmer to remove the fried dough strips to the kitchen paper-lined plate to drain off the excess oil. Whilst the dough strips are still hot, dunk each one in the coconut or brown sugar until coated all over.

Divide the hot sugar-coated dough strips between four serving plates. You can then either drizzle the chocolate sauce over the top with a spoon, or place the chocolate sauce in a serving bowl for people to dunk their own dough strips into. Serve the dough strips with some vegan whipped cream or single cream, if you like.

Index

Acknowledgements

We are grateful to our Marketing Manager and dear friend Rob Trounce for giving his time to read and edit our manuscript and for contributing to write this book. His passion and talent for describing Purezza's dishes have given the readers a true taste of Italy and an insight of the restaurant's most successful creations.

We thank Tara O'Sullivan and the team at Kyle Books for giving us the opportunity to produce this book and for being helpful and accommodating on various occasions.

A special thanks for their professional approach throughout all the photo shooting sessions goes to Faith Mason for the photography, Emily Jonzen for the food styling and Agathe Gits for the props.

We thank Paul Palmer-Edwards for the graphic design, whose work made it possible to achieve such an incredible result.

We are eternally grateful to those who have always believed in us and have supported and encouraged our plant-based project, in particular our families, loyal customers and followers, without whom Purezza would not exist.

We finally thank each other as authors for motivating and supporting each other, and for sharing the same values that help us move forward together as a team.